REMODELING
FOR
SECURITY

ABOUT THE AUTHOR

A. J. Harmon is a member of the American Institute of Architects and the National Council of Architectural Registration Boards, and has designed buildings in the United States, South America, Asia, Africa, and the Middle East. He has written a number of books on home remodeling and has been an editor for **Home Modernizing Guide** and **New Homes Guide.** His articles have appeared in such publications as **Better Homes and Gardens, Building Products Guide,** and **Popular Science.** He lives in Southampton, New York.

REMODELING
FOR
SECURITY

A.J. HARMON, A.I.A.

McGraw-Hill Book Company NEW YORK/ST. LOUIS/SAN FRANCISCO/MEXICO/TORONTO/DÜSSELDORF

123456789HAHA7832109

Library of Congress Cataloging in Publication Data

Harmon, Allen Jackson, date
Remodeling for security.
Includes index.
1. Dwellings—Remodeling.   2. Dwellings—
Security measures.   I. Title.
TH4816.H35   643   78-5059
ISBN 0-07-026627-1

The author would like to thank Robert Frank Lewis
for his assistance in the research, design, writing,
and drawings presented in this book

Contents

REMODELING
FOR
SECURITY

The thirteenth-century castle of Coucy is characteristic of the advanced type of military construction designed and built for security, with a central keep commanding a view of the valley. The top floors of the towers are projected so missiles could be dropped on besiegers below. Walls, sometimes 20 feet thick, were crenelated to protect archers who manned the walls. A moat and drawbridge protected the single entrance.

Chapter One

Security, Past and Present

In varying degrees, security has always been a part of the design of our homes throughout the history of architecture. As civilizations rose, flourished, and declined, the needs of security changed to protect people's homes from two recurring threats, those from outside the town and those from within the immediate neighborhood. A rising civilization must have fortifications and town walls to protect itself from invasion by enemies. As cultures advance, become more powerful and affluent, the sanctity of every man's home is respected and security becomes less important than beauty and convenience. During a decline, security takes on new meaning as man must protect himself, his family and possessions not only from his less fortunate neighbors, but from civil turmoil outside his door.

Historically, then, a civilization at the height of its power, with its people and property safe from outside attack, has been less concerned with security in the design of its dwellings than with style, comfort, and convenience. Yet some of architecture's most beautiful forms have evolved in times of turmoil or unrest, when residential design has had to provide for maximum security. Such innovations as courtyards, walled gardens, balconies, and roof gardens all had their genesis in the need for protection. Designing for security affected both castles and cottages. Many of these historical design concepts are still valid for consideration in our homes today.

Until the invention of gunpowder in the early fifteenth century made heavy fortifications obsolete, towns and castles were built with thick walls, moats, battlements, and drawbridges for protection against enemies, intruders, and marauding bands. After the fall of the Roman Empire there was a long

11

A typical Roman street in a walled town about the beginning
of the second half of the first century. Earlier and more
primitive houses such as those on the left were gradually torn
down and replaced with larger and more comfortable houses
and apartment buildings. Shops occupied many of the ground
floors, with living quarters grouped around secure interior
courtyards. Porches and balconies projected over the streets.

A. G. Harmon

Tower houses evolved during the Fall of Rome when there was widespread chaos throughout Europe and security precautions were left largely to the individual homeowner. Easier to defend than a walled villa, the tower house had a semi-public room on the ground floor protected by private guards.

period of chaos in Europe. The cities were in ruin, bands of Vandals roamed the countryside, and a new house form evolved due to the problems inherent in maintaining maximum security in houses with only walls to protect them. It was called a tower house.

The tower house was built up instead of out, and the first floor was a semipublic area and guard room. The upper floors of the house were reserved for the private apart-ments of the family. This type of concentrated structure was much easier to defend than the Roman villa spread out over a large area and became the form that was later developed in such buildings as the Tower of London. For a limited site, especially one with a view, and for increased security, the tower house is a valid possibility for some homes of today.

When Italy began to get back on its feet at

At the beginning of the Renaissance the fortified castle moved to town and became a city palace, as typified by the Palazzo Strozzi begun in Florence in 1489. Ground-floor windows were placed high in the rusticated masonry walls and were heavily barred. Upper-story windows were shuttered at night.

the beginning of the fifteenth century and the Renaissance, the old fortified castle had moved to town and become a town palace. It was secure from local threats and from wandering bandits and thieves. It would not have withstood a siege, but the masonry walls were heavy, the ceilings high, and regularly spaced windows appeared on each floor. At first, ground-floor windows were small, placed as high as possible in the wall, and always barred. As town security improved, the windows got larger, even those on the ground floor, but they remained heavily barred.

England, on the other hand, remained essentially an agricultural country, except for a few big cities like London, and the market towns grew unhampered over the countryside. After the fifteenth century it was useless to build castles and walls that could

easily be breached by cannon, and houses were being built with large leaded-glass windows in walls that would previously have been almost solid masonry.

By the time the Renaissance reached England, residential security in most areas was taken for granted. There was some crime, mostly confined to large cities, but both Henry VIII and his daughter Elizabeth I and their constables dealt harshly with offenders. People lived at ease in their country estates and cottages. By the time Hardwich Hall was completed in 1597, it was famous for its windows, and the people of Derbyshire used to quip, "Hardwick Hall, more glass than wall."

16 | REMODELING FOR SECURITY

Security in England in the early part of the Renaissance was of little concern, as exhibited in the design and construction of Hardwick Hall. This Elizabethan country house, begun in 1576, used vast amounts of glass, eliminating the defensive character of earlier keeps and castles. In many ways it is the forerunner of residential architecture as we know it today. The towers are decorated with scrollwork containing the initials ES for Elizabeth, Countess of Shrewsbury, also known as Bess of Hardwick.

A. J. Harmon

This tendency toward openness and light has continued to the point where homes and even banks are now being built with walls of nothing but glass. However, there has been a return to the need for greater architectural security, to the conditions that produced the closed and almost windowless facades of the Roman houses, the moated and fortified cas-tles of medieval Europe. Today we are facing a growing need to protect our families and possessions. In addition, our neighborhoods become more crowded, our homes and lives less private, we move farther and farther into the suburbs, abandoning established utilities, streets, transportation systems, and police protection. We have become a nation of movers, isolated people who scarcely know our next-door neighbors even though we may have lived next door to them for years. In going full circle in our search for privacy and security, we are returning to the fortified concept that every man's home is his castle.

Security has become such a vital concern in American society today that more and more homeowners are even arming themselves for their own protection. We have good laws, but we have too many of them and they are difficult to enforce. Police forces all over the country are finding it harder than ever to deal with robberies and burglaries. Most police organizations have established special offices to advise people how to make their homes more secure and safer from break-ins. Because of the almost overwhelming problems facing them, however, the police cannot handle the mounting crime rate against homeowners.

It is the purpose of this book to use the knowledge, experience, and successful concepts of the past to aid in solving the problems of today—to help you remodel your home as economically as possible for increased security and at the same time to improve the value and enhance the design of your own personal environment. In addition to being able to learn from the past, we can take advantage of machine-made materials and the latest discoveries of science and technology. In some ways the present era is an anomaly. Our civilization is flourishing, but the need for security continues to be a major factor in the design of our homes.

Medieval streets such as this exist throughout Europe and are a great attraction to American tourists. The half-timber houses and shops were cantilevered over the narrow street to save space in the walled town. Businesses were mixed with residential areas, so the street had a continuous flow of life through it all day and most of the evening.

Chapter Two

The Law and Legal Regulations

AGallup poll taken a few years ago showed that one American adult in eight—about 25,000,000—would prefer to live abroad. That is twice as many as in 1959, and three times as many as just after World War II. This trend may be reversing somewhat today, because European towns and cities are losing some of their charm to fiendish traffic jams, supermarkets, and to impersonal hotel chains as the "Americanizing" of Europe progresses. But there is still nothing that can compete with an Italian hill town. The grandeur of a Taormina, just one of the Greek-settled hill towns in Sicily, is breathtaking.

Every year thousands and thousands of Americans flock to Europe for the beauty of the countryside and the elegant charm of the architecture. They go because they can find in Europe what they cannot find at home: simple and beautiful architecture; clean, safe, quiet, romantic, tree-lined streets; country lanes strewn with flowers.

We have the capacity for this kind of charm in the United States, but we are often hampered by restrictive zoning ordinances. The Romans were the great city planners of all time. They planned and built cities on a scale and with an intelligence superior to ours today. A great deal of consideration was given to water supply, sewage, security, and to the industry that the surrounding farmland could ecologically support. They had a very effective means of control: when the population reached a predetermined number, further expansion was prohibited, and another city was planned and built in a suitable location, elsewhere.

Within the city walls, the blocks or sections were also planned—but not with the rigid restrictions that can produce

The Spanish village of Os de Civis near Andorra in the Pyrenees clustered around the church. Protected by the mountains, with a clear view of the valley below, this could be any one of a number of beautiful and fascinating hill towns in Europe.

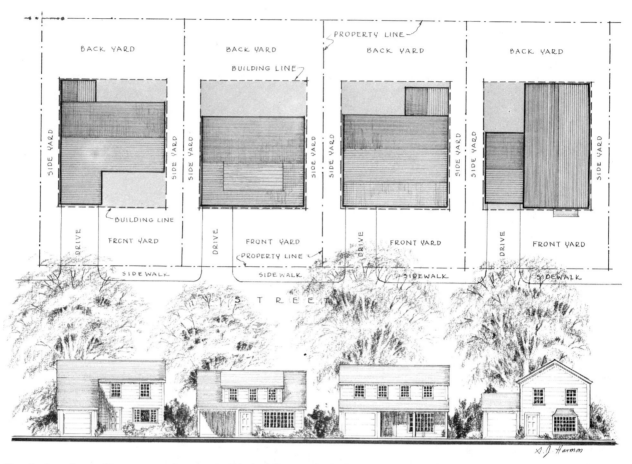

Standard zoning ordinances restrict permissible building areas, indicated by shaded areas. On suburban streets like this, such laws often produce useless front yards open to the public, narrow passages between houses, allowing access to back yards by strangers, and very little privacy from house to house.

the crippling waste of a present-day financial district such as Wall Street, which is teeming during the day and completely deserted at night and on weekends. To be sure, there were specific sections for specific markets (one for fish, located near the river, another for fruits and vegetables near the gate to the farmland, another for grain, and bread bakeries, as well as streets for workers of brass, for silver, and so on), but houses and apartments were mixed with shops and businesses, so streets were used constantly.

Eventually our own laws will have to be changed to allow more effective and efficient land use. Current set-back regulations in towns and cities are wasteful, not only of land, but of construction materials and water, sewer, and electric lines. Urban and suburban sprawl means longer trips to the office and supermarkets, which in turn increases the demand for highway construction and gasoline.

Not all building regulations are bad, however. Most towns and cities in the United States have some zoning ordinances and building codes that regulate construction and remodeling. Basically these regulations are designed to protect you, your family, and your property and must be complied with when you remodel.

Before you begin your remodeling, investigate the deed restrictions, zoning ordinances, and building codes that are in force in your area. You should also talk to the local police and see what they can recommend to make your house more secure.

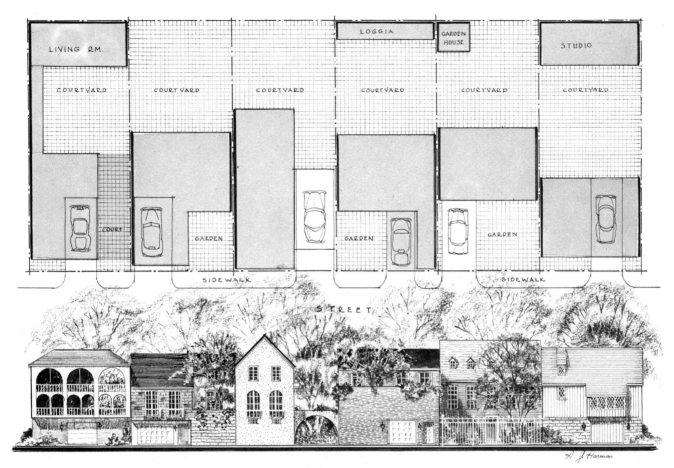

More creative zoning ordinances would permit better use of space, utilities, and streets. High fences and garden walls protect windows, gardens, and courtyards. Balconies and raised porches permit outdoor relaxation in safety even at night.

DEED RESTRICTIONS

Deed restrictions are conditions written into the deed to your property at the time of purchase to maintain a certain standard of excellence in the neighborhood. Since they may supersede less strict zoning ordinances, you should reread your deed carefully and inform the architect, or whoever is planning the remodeling, of any restrictions.

Deed restrictions can limit the use of certain materials, determine the basic type of construction, and could conceivably even determine the color you are permitted to paint the exterior of your house. The style of architecture, for example, may have to conform to that already existing in the neighborhood. If all the houses in the area are Georgian or Cape Cod, you can be prohibited from remodeling your home in a glass-walled, flat-roofed, Bauhaus style.

These restrictions are designed to maintain the character of the neighborhood. They can be dogmatic, but with intelligent interpretation they can be responsible for creating a consistent neighborhood with stabilized property values.

ZONING ORDINANCES

These laws restrict and define the use of land and buildings for residences, business, and industry. Zoning ordinances, unlike deed re-

Deed restrictions serve to maintain the character of the neighborhood. They can prohibit the construction of a building out of keeping with the generally accepted standards—such as this modern house in an area of traditionally styled houses.

strictions, are almost always written for the homeowner's protection to prevent adjacent and nearby property from being turned into gasoline stations, rooming houses, trailer parks, or anything else that would decrease the value of your home as a private residence.

Zoning also regulates the number of families permitted to live in one house. Some ordinances allow two-family homes, while others can prevent you from renting out an apartment in your house unless you are in residence as the owner. Some areas are so strictly zoned that only one family, and a kitchen, are permitted on the site. These laws are meant to protect the neighborhood from rooming houses and apartments that might strain the water supply, sewage systems, and municipal services. They are also a check on overcrowding.

The percentage of the lot that can be built on is usually regulated, along with minimum footage for front, side, and back yards. The height of walls and fences is also usually controlled, so if you are considering having a chain-link fence or wall put up, check with the local zoning ordinances first.

You may consider some of these regulations restrictive, but zoning also prevents the construction of chicken coops, stables, outhouses, billboards, or anything that would constitute a neighborhood nuisance. Automobile parking is usually regulated so that the street will not be blocked by cars that might prevent a fire truck or ambulance from getting through in case of an emergency.

A copy of the zoning ordinance is usually available at the town hall or building inspector's office, and you should check it before you build walls or fences or plan your remodeling. Unless you obtain a variance beforehand, any illegal construction can be removed and you can be subject to a fine.

Zoning ordinances may prevent the construction of gasoline or service stations, the conversion of an existing structure into a roominghouse, or anything else that could constitute a neighborhood nuisance.

VARIANCE

If you think that the zoning ordinance governing something that you want to do is too restrictive, you can apply to your town's zoning board to have the ordinance waived in your particular case. This waiver is called a variance.

As a security measure, for instance, you may want to fence in your yard, but the allowable four-foot height of a fence will not give you the security you desire. Then you apply for a variance. The zoning board of appeals meets periodically to review just such cases. Usually a solution can be worked out to everyone's satisfaction.

BUILDING CODES

Each section of a town is regulated by a zoning ordinance and each building within that section must conform to a building code that is designed to protect public health and safety. For private houses, the code specifies minimum sizes for beams and columns and other structural members. It can control the design of roofs to prevent them from blowing off in a high wind or collapsing under a snow load. The code also regulates the construction of chimneys, the installation of furnaces, and the storage of fuel and gasoline so houses do not become firetraps.

Plumbing systems are also regulated to ensure that sanitary conditions are of the highest quality, not only to protect your own home, but also to protect you from faulty plumbing problems due to a neighbor's negligence. The same is true of all electrical work. As with the plumbing, electrical work must be overseen by a building inspector during the remodeling to protect your family from electric shock and fires caused by defective wiring.

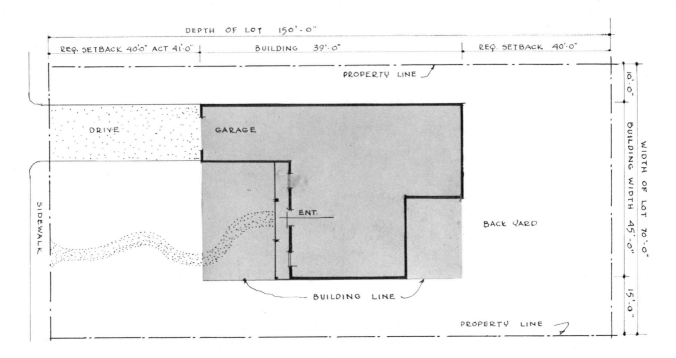

The standard site plan of a suburban property. The allowable building area is shaded; any construction within this area may be as high as the house. Any construction, including fences, outside this area requires a variance, with the exception of terraces, paths, and paving.

The building code establishes only minimum safety requirements and should not be used as a guide for excellence. Plumbers and electricians must be licensed, and if your remodeling is extensive enough to require a building permit, the code will require them to take out separate permits for their work. Some communities will allow you to do the plumbing and electrical work on your own house. If you do, you also should conform to the building code, not only for your own safety but as a precaution in case of an accident and insurance claim. Some insurance companies will not honor claims if the work done on the house was substandard. The building code was written for your protection. Both the building code and the building inspectors can be of help to you; and they should not be considered as obstacles to be avoided.

BUILDING INSPECTOR

If you are required to obtain a building permit (and in some communities just a chain-link fence requires one), a building inspector must be called in. If there are any plumbing or electrical changes, he must approve each stage of the work. Even if you do not need a permit and are going to be doing the work yourself, a building inspector can be a good source of information and advice.

BUILDING PERMIT

Each community has its own criterion for demanding a building permit. If you are required to have a building permit, drawings of the proposed changes must be submitted to the building department, which will check

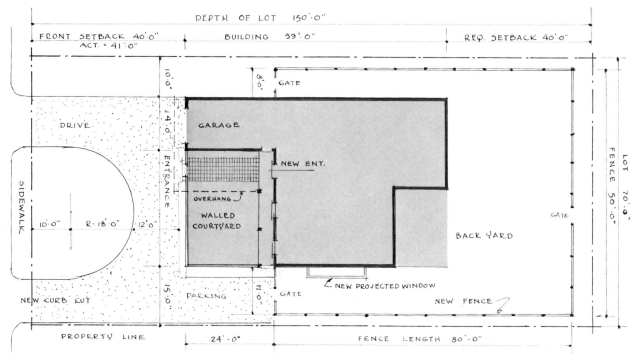

To apply for a variance a detailed plot plan must be submitted to local authorities for their approval. In this case the site is wide enough to provide for a circular drive, which may require a variance because of the additional curb cut. The walled courtyard has been designed within the building line.

them to see that everything you propose conforms to the zoning ordinances and building codes.

You may need a building permit for any major structural changes or additions that require new plumbing or wiring. New windows, an alarm system, new doors, locks, a new kitchen, or enclosing a porch would probably not require building permits because they are improvements that occur within the existing structure. However, adding on to the house or erecting a high fence or wall to enclose a terrace or the garden could require a building permit and, theoretically at least, you would not be allowed to use the new space until a building inspector issued a certificate of occupancy (usually referred to simply as a CO).

If you are in doubt as to whether you need a building permit for your remodeling, consult the building-permit authorities in your community. When you apply for a permit, you will be asked to pay a fee based on the anticipated cost of construction. It can take from one to three weeks for the plans to be checked and to receive the permit, which must be displayed prominently on the house.

CERTIFICATE OF OCCUPANCY

The certificate of occupancy is issued only after the building inspector, having approved each stage of the construction, is satisfied that it has been completed according to the plans filed with his office when the building permit was issued. A copy of the certificate is also sent to the tax department, so you can expect to pay an increased property tax reflecting the increased value of your house.

A New England saltbox, typical of those houses that were built with unskilled labor in the Colonies in the seventeenth century, following basic design and construction practices brought from Europe. The house derived its name from the shed so often added at a later date, giving the appearance of the boxes every kitchen of the day used to hold the precious salt.

Chapter Three

Getting the Work Done

From the earliest days of our settlement, Americans have had a penchant for remodeling and adding to their homes, and two of our indigenous styles, the standard colonial and the saltbox, have evolved to provide for just that. A two-story colonial house has a center-hall design with the entrance in the middle of the facade. On the first floor there are two windows on each side of the door, and on the second floor, there are five windows, centered on the windows and door below. The saltbox design is a compact two-story structure with a lean-to shed added at the back. It is called a saltbox because, with the added shed on the rear, it resembles the old tin saltboxes kept in every settler's kitchen.

In the early post-log-cabin days when you needed a house but did not want or could not afford a whole one, what you generally got was a half house or a three-quarter house that became a colonial or a saltbox, depending on the direction in which you expanded as your family and finances increased. Certain regions had their own style of house, such as the Cape Cod, and when you lived there and wanted a house, that was what you got.

This seemingly casual system of design and construction had, and still has, great economic advantages. The same concept was adopted by Henry Ford in the manufacturing of automobiles: When you bought a car, it was a Ford and it was black.

Many countries today still use these basic concepts of design and building, with results both economical and aesthetically satisfying. There is no need to deal with architects, preliminary designs, and involved legal agreements with lawyers and contractors. In an Italian village, for example, if you want a house

Half house

Three-quarter house

American Colonial houses as they developed without skilled labor, designers, or architects. Security became less of a problem in the eighteenth century and the gardens settled around the house, but even as they did, iron fences and gates protected the grounds, marking the public from the private areas of the house.

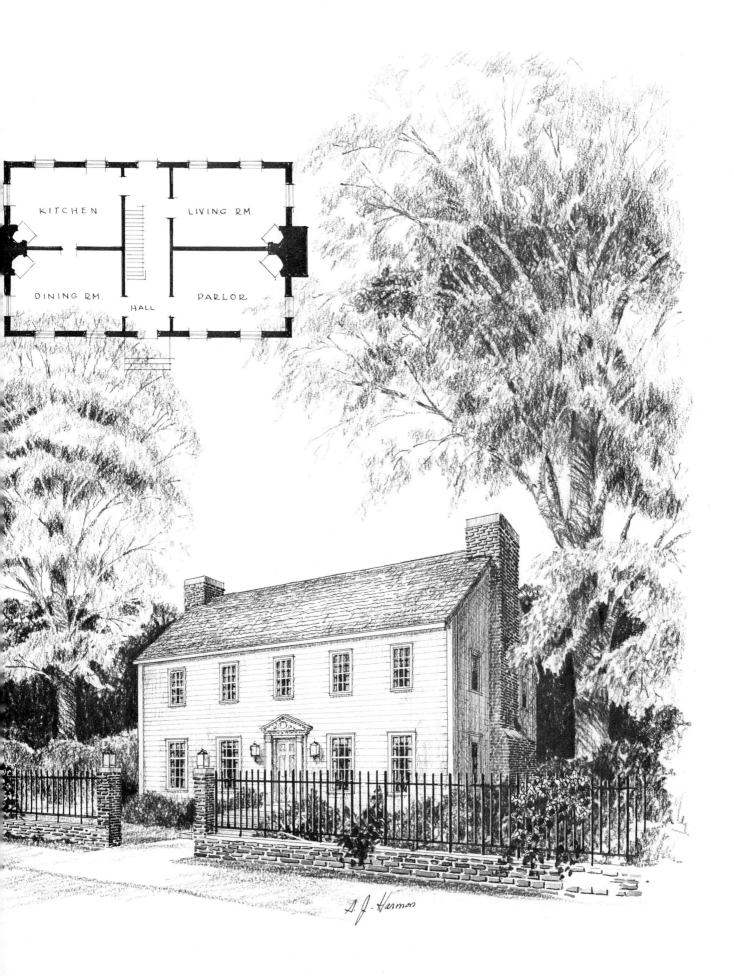

KITCHEN LIVING RM.

DINING RM. PARLOR

HALL

A.J.Harmon

A beautiful concept of a secure rural farmhouse near Lucca, Italy. Built of native materials and labor in the design favored in the region, the once-stuccoed masonry exterior is now practically worn away by wind and weather. Farm animals, equipment, and storage occupied the ground floor while family living rooms and bedrooms were placed above and opened onto large safe loggias.

you point to where you want it built and tell the local mason how many rooms you want. In Japan you just tell the carpenter how many tatamis you want on the floor. In the city certain rules are followed, usually known only to the builder, and in the country you get the kind of house that is built in the region. An Italian builder may make a few changes from time to time in the arches of the arcade or the mason may add an extra balconied window if he likes the view of a particular olive grove. In Japan the exact design of the tokonoma, or "honored spot," may change if the carpenter finds an especially attractive tree trunk he wants to incorporate in the treatment. By and large the builder will give you the best he can with the materials that are available.

In the United States, building and remodeling have become a more complex matter.

Another Italian farmhouse near Siena, reflecting the local building design using unplastered stone, with family living quarters raised safely above the ground level. The houses shown on these pages are not the country retreats of wealthy landowners, but were owned and built by craftsmen in the area.

Making your home more secure is going to involve more than simply fitting a better lock on the front door and putting up a fence along the lot line. Of course, a lock can help to make your house harder to break into if the door itself is heavy and in good shape, but a new lock on a poor door is wasted money. A four-foot-high fence will define your property line, but it is not going to keep anybody out who wants in. And neither the lock nor the fence is necessarily going to make your house more attractive.

When you are making security improvements to your home, you may be capable of doing all the carpentry, painting, and other work required, but if the effort is not centered around a good design, your labors will have been wasted. The elements to be considered are materials, lighting, ventilation, access, circulation, convenience, security,

Even with the plastered walls roughed by weather, this securely built farmhouse outside Arezzo, Italy, has lost none of its dignity adapted by local masons from a remembered classical model.

beauty, and how all of these can increase the value of your property.

You may think you know all about design and construction, but most people find as the work goes along that they need professional help. This is not to suggest that if you want to put a fence around the yard you have to go out and hire an architect, contractor, and landscape gardener, but neither should you avoid professional help and advice. Sometimes a simple, and seemingly offhand, remark by an architect can save you money and improve the security of your home. For instance, he may point out a cheaper, more attractive way of building a fence or mention that, although the plastic you were going to use to replace the glass in

the French doors is tough to break, it melts from the heat of a match or simple blowtorch.

THE ARCHITECT

You may think that you do not need an architect to design and supervise the security remodeling for your home, and you may be right, but the best way to find out is to let him tell you. An architect is not necessarily going to save you money, as he will work within the budget you set up, but he will see that you get the most for what you have to spend. The amount of the budget is no indi-

In this typical farmhouse near Arezzo, Italy, masonry visible through the deteriorating stucco only adds to the appearance of strength. Bars on the lower windows of the stalls and storage rooms provide both light and security.

cation as to whether you need an architect or not. In fact, the less money you have, the more important it is to spend it wisely.

An architect will plan, design, find the best contractors, and supervise the security work for you. If you plan to do the work yourself, he can provide the design and expert advice on the best way to do things with the least expensive materials.

WORKING WITH AN ARCHITECT

Finding an architect is not difficult. Finding one who will take on a small remodeling job can take a little time. Call or write to the local chapter of the American Institute of Architects (A.I.A.) and ask for the names of members in your area who do residential work. Or you can find registered architects in the Yellow Pages of your telephone book. Call several who are nearby and tell them your problem. Those who cannot take on the job will know and recommend someone who is qualified.

Make a rough floor plan of the house and take it with photographs when you go to talk to the architect. Draw your own design solution and ask him to criticize it and make suggestions. This is a good way to indicate to him the scope of the work and what you have in mind. He may be able to show you in a rough sketch the best solution.

An architect may not charge you for a short talk in his office, but if he spends much time coming to the house and giving you sketches, do not expect him to work for nothing. Ask first. His fee is usually based on a percentage of the cost of the work, but he can also work on a set fee established in advance, or on an hourly or daily basis. The contract can be a standard A.I.A. form or a simple letter of agreement.

If you are going to do the work yourself, perhaps all you will need from the architect is a quick sketch and advice on materials and how to get started. If you are going to call in a contractor for plumbing, electrical, or carpentry work, ask the architect's advice on the best contractors for the work you want done. He will have worked with them before and will know who is reliable and who is not.

THE CONTRACTOR

General contractors, as they are called, organize the remodeling, get permits, order materials, schedule and supervise the subcontractors—the plumber, electrician, mason, roofer, carpenter, tile setter, painter, and so on. If you do not have an architect and cannot do the work yourself, finding a good contractor can take months.

Question everyone you know who has had any work done within the last five years and ask them whom they used and about the quality of the work and promptness in getting it done. Many contractors and subcontractors may be willing to do the work, but very few will complete it when they say they will. You can spend weeks in frustrated anticipation waiting for them to show up.

You can call local architects and ask whom they would recommend to do the work, but they may be reluctant to give you the names of their best men since good con-

tractors are hard to find and booked up long in advance. It is better to compile a list of possible contractors in advance and ask the architects which ones they think would do the best job.

Checking with the Better Business Bureau is for the most part a waste of time. They can only tell you if complaints have been lodged against any of their members, and joining the Bureau is not compulsory. Lumberyards, building supply companies, banks, and local building departments usually do not want to become involved in recommending one contractor over another. Aside from the recommendations of friends or an architect, an excellent local reputation is probably the best criterion for hiring a contractor you can trust.

WORKING WITH A CONTRACTOR

Once you have found several contractors you think can do the work, give them all identical sketches and specifications, and let each know that you are getting estimates from other contractors. If, after you get back several bids, the contractor you like the most has submitted the highest bid, ask him if he cannot meet one of the more reasonable bids.

Be very careful about accepting the lowest or highest bid. The lowest bidder can be either desperate or incompetent, and the highest can be uninterested in doing the work.

Have your lawyer draw up an agreement with the contractor that includes the specifications, the dated sketch you gave the contractor for his bid if it remains the same, and a work schedule showing when the workmen will arrive to begin the work and the date on which the work will be finished under a "time is of the essence" clause. Agree to nothing verbally.

If you can, have the contractor give you a schedule showing when the plumbing and electricity are going to be turned on and off so you can make arrangements accordingly.

Get furniture, carpets, draperies, and knickknacks out of the contractor's way. He is a builder, not a mover. Keep pets and children away from the workmen and their tools, and never ask them to baby-sit while you run to the supermarket. Do not follow the contractor or his men around asking questions, and never make any changes unless they are absolutely necessary and the price is agreed to in writing.

Pay the contractor according to the contract, but only for labor and materials that have been installed. Make the final payment only after the contractor's work has been completed to your satisfaction, since the contractor may otherwise fail to return to install a missing latch or to repair defective work.

SUBCONTRACTORS

If you cannot find a general contractor you can trust to do the work, you can have the remodeling done by subcontractors you hire yourself. You can also save money by subcontracting the work, but it will not be done as quickly because the subcontractors will have to schedule your work between larger jobs they have with contractors and builders. This is to be expected, because the subcontractors depend on these sources for consistent employment and may work for you only once.

Unless you are going to do your own carpentry, the best place to start is with a good carpenter. Good carpenters are harder to find than good contractors, and they are expensive, but worth it. The carpenter, who will have worked with all the other trades, will know the best men for the jobs you want done and can be helpful in coordinating the schedules.

If you decide to do the carpentry yourself, you will have to use the process of elimination to hire the other trades you need. Do not hire any of these people as employees or you will be responsible for withholding Social Security and income taxes and paying workmen's compensation and unemployment insurance.

Before entering into any agreements with subcontractors, talk to your insurance agent to be sure that you are fully covered in case of an accident. When the remodeling is completed, have the agent increase your insurance to cover the cost of the improvements.

Unplanned and poorly designed security remodeling can turn a classic house, such as the one on page 31, into the unhappy result pictured here. Secure enough perhaps, but ugly and uncomfortable. Metal awning windows are safe, but out of character, as are the dormers, entrance, garage, and kitchen addition.

Chapter Four

Saving, Budgeting, Financing

With an unlimited amount of money available to you, almost anything can be done to make your house or apartment more secure. But not many people are in a position to order anything they want without careful scrutiny of the right-hand column. Even then, an expensive dinner is no guarantee of a good one. Spending a lot of money to make your house more secure does not necessarily make it so.

Neither does spending freely offer any assurance that your home will be more attractive.

How many times have you been invited to a friend's house to see a new prized possession that turns out to be something that made you wonder who in the world would buy such a thing when you saw it advertised? Well, someone must like those statues of naked ladies with clocks in their navels or they would not be manufactured. There is no such thing as "good taste," whether it applies to our clothing or our homes. Its application should be reserved for the palate. (You don't have to guess whether a fish has gone bad or not—you know.) Good taste is a matter of knowing what is right for you. It is the only thing that will produce the results you want and can afford.

The very best way to waste a lot of money and come up with something you do not like and that does not work is to do a bit of haphazard remodeling in one place this year and some more in another place next year without considering the overall design of the house. You could find that the bathroom you added last year is in exactly the perfect location for the new entrance and drive you want to add this year. Only the wealthy can afford to make mistakes or change their minds and have work taken out and done over.

It is strange that many people readily admit they do not

Regardless of how attractive the neighborhood may be, there is always the tendency in remodeling to invest more than you can get out of the property if circumstances force you to sell. This is called "overbuilding the neighborhood." Not only is it financially risky, but inadvisable from a security standpoint; if you were a burglar, which house would you choose?

A. J. Harmon

Plan and elevation of a classic house as remodeled for security by an architect, in contrast to the same house on page 38 remodeled without professional help. Pantry, laundry, bath, kitchen entrance, and garage have been added to form a walled court off the dining room.

know how to cook or sew, but few will admit that they do not know what is best for their house—as if being brought up in one or owning one qualifies them as expert. It is much the same as expecting a driver's license to entitle one to be a competent mechanic.

Very few people would sit down one weekend and begin cutting into a fabric that cost $300 a yard to recover the sofa unless they were expert and experienced upholsterers. That is about what our houses cost today per square yard, and yet we cut into them carelessly.

Do not try to save money by avoiding professional help. If you do not know exactly what you want or how to get it, have an architect draw up a plan for your remodeling and stick with it. Design and planning are more important than the best materials and the highest-quality craftsmanship. These mean nothing if they are not well incorporated to contribute to the best possible solution.

You do not have to do all remodeling at once. What is essential in budgeting the remodeling is that each stage be complete in

Perspective of house from the street with a chain-link fence. The addition of concrete supports and rosebushes softens the starkness of the fence while increasing security.

itself and that it contribute without change to the projects anticipated for the following years. Saving money is not a question of not spending it, but a matter of spending it well.

THE NEIGHBORHOOD

A common, if very human, mistake when we remodel our homes is to spend more than we can get out of them if, for some reason, we are forced to sell them. This is called overbuilding the neighborhood. Zoning or-

dinances prohibit the construction of walls and structure outside a given area of the lot and state the minimum square footage a new house must have on the first floor. But the zoning ordinances establish only minimums. Certain maximums are conformed to because of our regimented concepts of real estate.

If you buy or build a house in a neighborhood of $40,000 houses and spend another $40,000 remodeling and improving the grounds, you might get $50,000 or $60,000 for it if you had to sell. It could take quite a

Any attempt to improve security at the entrance is wasted unless sliding glass doors around the corner are also protected. Another security risk is the low eave and the shallow angle of the rear addition, which make second-floor windows easily accessible.

long time to find a buyer, however, and you would still lose up to $30,000 of your investment.

We love our own children (no matter how unattractive they may be to others) and want the best for them, but that sentiment should stop there and not be carried over to our houses. Our homes reflect our lives and personalities, and it can be very reassuring to know we have the best house on the block. But when it is also the most expensive, it can cease to be a source of pride and become a nagging responsibility. And, again,

the most expensive is not always the best.

Before you begin to remodel, get an accurate evaluation of your home's worth in relation to that of other property in the neighborhood. Real estate people may be of some help, but you should also talk to a mortgage banker, a contractor, an architect, to see what houses are selling for in your area. Keep your spending down so that your total investment is well within the lowest figure, either by doing much of the work yourself or by pacing the improvement stages so that as prices and values rise you can remain on the

Remodeling one area of the house for security can be defeated by a porch enclosed by jalousie windows and doors.

lower side of the general price range of your neighbors.

THE HOUSE

There is also such a thing as "overbuilding the house." This is overimproving one area of the property or house while neglecting another. In remodeling for security, this could mean enclosing the yard and garden with an expensive brick wall when the doors and windows need replacing and the house needs a new roof or insulation. It could mean adding a new garage when the house actually needs another bathroom.

Improve the entire property and not just an isolated part of it. Achieve an overall consistent level of improvement that combines maintenance and remodeling.

DOORS

Old paneled exterior doors or insecure doors with glass in the upper section need not be

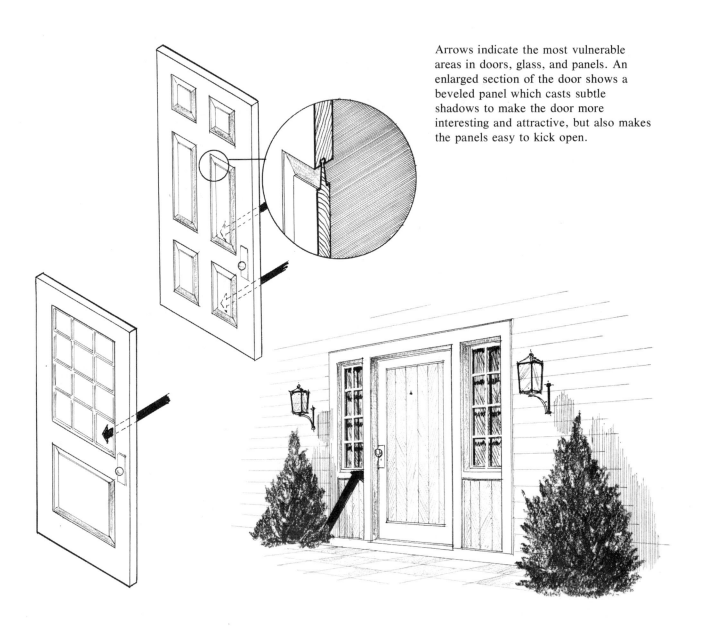

Arrows indicate the most vulnerable areas in doors, glass, and panels. An enlarged section of the door shows a beveled panel which casts subtle shadows to make the door more interesting and attractive, but also makes the panels easy to kick open.

thrown away. If they are basically sound, they can be saved and reused elsewhere or reinforced and remodeled. Often, in older homes, uneven settling over the years may have twisted the door frames out of plumb. Even if the original doors have been adjusted from time to time so they fit well, they may need more secure protection.

The glass in upper sections of exterior doors can easily be broken to get at the lock. The same is true of sidelights and panels. In most standard paneled doors, the panels have been beveled to produce a more attractive door and are so thin at the edges

they can be pushed out or broken through with little more than a good kick.

This is partly because times were different when the houses were built; security was not the problem it is today, and all the door had to do was keep the air out. The doors were also built of solid wood, which can be carved to make them more interesting, but because the grain of the wood goes all the way through, the paneling can be brittle.

If the jambs of the door frame are not rabbeted—that is, actually cut away to receive the door—they should be replaced. Door stops that are simply nailed on to hold

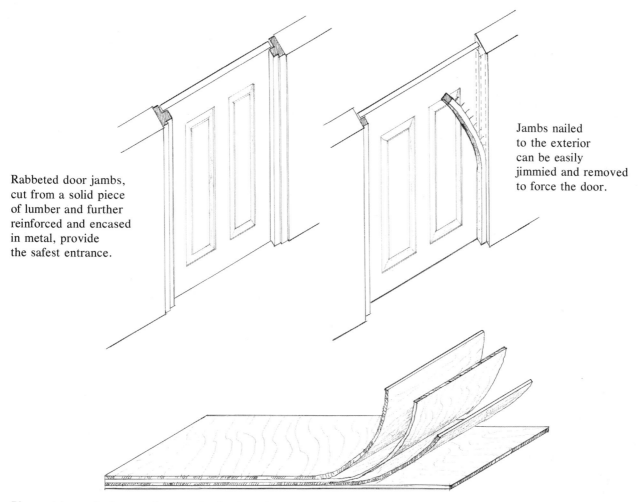

Rabbeted door jambs, cut from a solid piece of lumber and further reinforced and encased in metal, provide the safest entrance.

Jambs nailed to the exterior can be easily jimmied and removed to force the door.

Plywood is much stronger than regular lumber of the same thickness because it is glued together, with the grain in the alternate layers going in different directions.

the door can be removed quickly with a screwdriver. The doors should fit snugly in the frames and not rattle or they can easily be forced or jimmied. So get the frames in shape before getting new locks or replacing the doors.

Old doors can be refinished to fortify them on one or both sides with exterior grade plywood covering the glass and the panels. Modern plywood, made out of many thin layers of wood glued together, with the grains running at right angles to each other on every layer, is much tougher than solid wood of the same thickness.

The thicker the exterior plywood the better, but a minimum thickness of a half inch is recommended for both the exterior and interior of the door. The interior finish can be made of lighter paneling if the difference is made up on the outside.

The door must be taken out of its frame, and the plywood should be both glued and screwed to the surfaces. Nails (even with glue) are not nearly as strong as screws and will not prevent the plywood from being stripped off the door. New hinges will be needed to carry the additional weight, and the door should be fitted with a heavier mor-

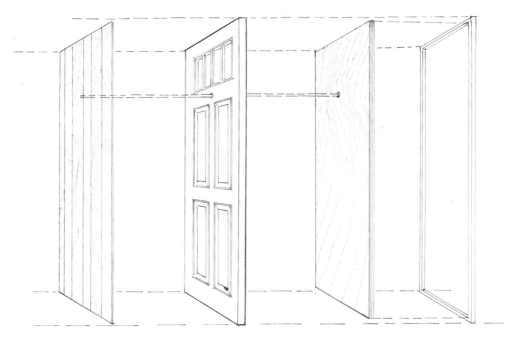

Exterior-grade ½-inch-thick plywood, surfaced on one side, can be used to reinforce the outside of old, insecure, or glazed doors. Thin finished paneling can be used to surface the interior side. A small frame of hardwood can surround the exterior plywood to cover and protect the edges. The plywood should be fastened to the door with glue and screws. A peephole at eye level will allow you to see who is at the door before opening it.

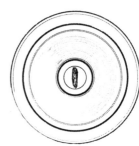

A temporary buttress bar can be placed under the knob of an old door and also taken with you when you travel, for use in hotel and motel rooms.

Cheap builder-grade "key-in-the knob" locks can be broken off with a twist and should be replaced at once with a mortised lock set with a dead bolt.

tise lock and dead bolt. A new doorknob will also be required if there are no extensions for the spindle. However, locks do wear out, and it is better to start with a new lock sized to fit the door without any leeway.

Do not try to save money on a cheap lock. The builder key-in-the-knob locks provide no security at all and can be forced with a screwdriver or simply twisted by hand until they grind and break. Some are so inadequate that if leaned on with a good shoulder they either break at the plate or the strike plate is pulled away from the jamb.

Since all doors open into the house, pushing the strike plate out of the door jamb can be quite easy if it is not set with long screws.

Putting heavy reinforcing plywood on the surface of the door is a simple process. Installing a new lock and hinges is not quite so easy. It is not a complicated process, although some tools and skill are required, but you may want to hire a carpenter for an hour instead of spending a day of your own time whittling away at what can be a frustrating task. The result can be a more secure door and a better-looking entrance.

Just a few of the well-designed doors that can sometimes be found in demolition yards and secondhand furniture stores, often with many layers of paint concealing beautiful carving and wood. Styles can vary from Spanish, English, Italian, to Early American and colonial.

Through quirks in carpentry and individualism, even new doors must be carefully planed and fitted, and they can still stick and bind from warping and swelling after a year or more. Instead of going to the expense of a new door if the existing one is beyond repair, look for a used door. Junk and salvage yards and often contractors will have beautiful old doors from demolished buildings that you can buy for less than half the price of an ugly new one.

You may have to cut the door down a bit to fit, but old doors have the advantages of being well dried out and of better quality wood and workmanship. You will not get the swelling and warping that can play havoc with weatherstripping. Some of the most attractive and interesting doors are from old banks and churches.

Double doors, always a bad security risk, can be improved inexpensively and without changing the character too much by making one of the doors stationary. The stationary door will have to be cut down so that a rabbeted three-inch by six-inch piece can be placed to receive the strike plate of the new

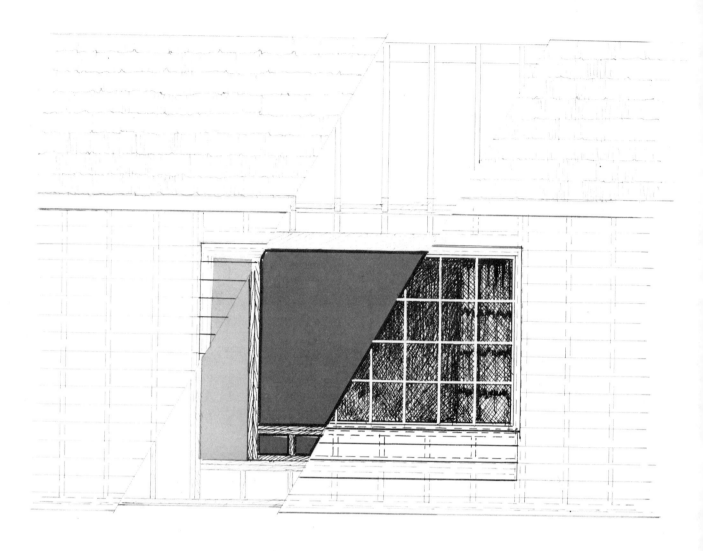

New secure windows (dark gray) replacing old windows (light gray) will usually have to be of a smaller size and will require new stud support and refinishing of interior and exterior wall surfaces on at least two sides.

lock. If the door is already fitted with a mortise lock and dead bolt, the stationary door will need to be held in place only with heavy stops screwed to the floor and head jambs.

For a rented apartment or as a temporary measure in a house with a weak lock, you can use a buttress lock, which is a four-foot metal bar bracketed off the door and the floor at an angle. A rubber wedge under the bottom of the door will not be nearly as effective, but it can be used as a temporary measure or possibly in motel doors when traveling. A shopkeeper's bell hung on the inside of the door will wake you at night if anyone should try the door hard enough to jar it.

WINDOWS

Windows not only are much more difficult to rehabilitate than doors but can also cause a greater security problem. Not only can the glass be broken to gain entry, but window sashes are made of much lighter material than doors. Buying new ones to fit existing frames is not easy either, because the sizes of windows change constantly and from one

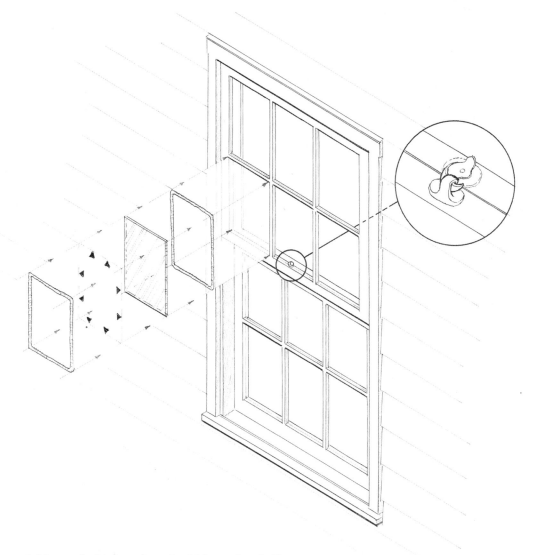

Old putty and thin, easily broken glass should be replaced. First a new, pencil-thin line of putty is applied. Then the glass pane is pressed into place, held with glazier's points, and another line of putty smoothed flat with a putty knife. The enlarged circled area shows a typical insecure window latch that can be forced open in a matter of seconds.

manufacturer to another, while door sizes, regulated by code and convention, remain relatively constant. Windows cannot be cut down in size as doors can, so you will always have to settle for a smaller size if the exact size cannot be matched. This means expensive filling and matching on at least two sides, plus new painting and trim.

The trouble with most old windows, both metal and wood, is that the glass is held in place with glazier's points—small triangular-shaped nails in wood windows and metal clips on metal windows—and putty. Both the glazier's points and the putty are applied from the exterior. Anything applied from the outside can be removed from the outside, creating a target for burglars and prowlers.

There are various kinds of putty. None of them is infallible, and all need to be replaced from time to time. When the putty starts to deteriorate, it can be picked away from the sash with a penknife or a nail. In such cases, intruders do not have to break the glass to enter; they can simply remove it to get to the locks. Windows with loose putty are a signal to the burglar that they may be in bad repair and that the locks may be slipped easily from the outside.

Secondhand shutters nailed over old windows can improve security, but should not be nailed over bedroom windows.

An old picture window can be made more secure and more attractive with used shutters.

Homemade shutters of secondhand planks can secure an old window, leaving the transom uncovered for light and air.

Ground-floor windows can be secured with shutters from the bottom up, bedroom and second-floor windows from the top down.

You can deter a prowler by keeping the windows puttied, in good shape with a snug fit, and secured with a key lock. The old twist locks supplied with windows are simple to open from the outside.

When you replace old windows, buy those that do not use putty to hold the glass in place. There are a number available at prices very little higher than the old-fashioned puttied type. Even the new ones, however, still have the old locks, so an additional one will have to be placed on each new window.

If your windows are a lost cause but you cannot afford to have them all replaced at once, you can nail inexpensive secondhand shutters over all or a portion of them (except for bedroom windows, which should never be sealed off; you must not prevent escape in an emergency).

Colonial houses and other examples of classical architecture do require windows suitable to their styles, but if you are not bound by this stricture you can replace insecure windows with sturdy wood frames, divided into small enough sections and heavy enough to discourage an adult from climbing

A classic facade, as on page 31, can be ruined by inappropriate windows that produce a blank, staring appearance.

An old window made secure with two-by-fours subdividing the surface into smaller areas.

A large glass area subdivided by two-by-fours and industrial wire for reinforcing.

through them even if the glass is broken away. One or more of the sections can be opened for ventilation, and with careful thought to the design, a new character can be given to the exterior of the house. Again, this is not suitable for bedroom windows.

In bedrooms old windows can be made more secure without sacrificing safety by surrounding them with secondhand shutters on the inside, leaving enough of the window exposed from top to bottom for a child to signal for help. The shutters can be removed from the inside by lifting them off closed brackets that an intruder would not know of and could not reach noiselessly. In an emergency an adult could pry the shutters away from the supports for a quick rescue from the exterior.

Some old windows, if not the standard colonial sash, are at best unattractive to begin with and the glass in them can be replaced by wire glass. While wire glass in itself is considered ugly by some, it will not detract from an already homely window. In fact, it can rather improve it because the eye is drawn to the wire and not the window. In-

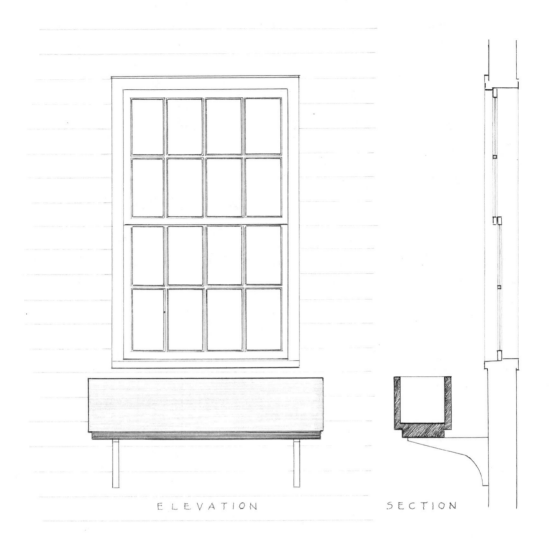

E L E V A T I O N   S E C T I O N

A window box, shown in elevation and section, can help make windows more secure by placing distance between window and intruder.

stead of using putty when the windows are reglazed, use glue, wood screws, caulking, and a sturdy wood stop to hold the glass in place and to waterproof the window.

Window boxes bolted to heavy brackets under and in front of the windows will keep prowlers away. To get through the window a burglar would have to navigate the window box and take a chance of its crashing down with him, creating a noticeable disturbance.

An imperceptible wire on the box attached to a bell on the inside of the house will notify occupants if the window box and windows are being tampered with. Leave a space between the box and the house wall large enough to see through but not large enough for an intruder to stand in or reach the window through.

The least expensive, but effective, double-hung window lock is a hole drilled through the sash large enough to hold a good-sized nail on both sides of the window. The nails must fit snugly and holes for them should be drilled in several locations so the window can be secured when open for ventilation. If you go away on a long trip, the window can be secured with a screw placed in the holes.

Shown in perspective, this window box not only makes the window more secure, but softens the facade.

FINANCING

The best, and usually the least expensive, way to pay for remodeling is in cash. However, this is not always possible and sometimes not advisable, depending on how you have your money invested. If it is in a good stock, the stock may go up more in several years than the interest you will have to pay on a loan you take out to finance the remodeling.

The worst, and most expensive, way to finance a security improvement on your home is to buy it from a salesman canvassing the neighborhood. He may be selling burglar alarm systems, for example, from door to door. He may tell you that he represents an old reliable firm just getting started in your area, and he would like to use your house as a neighborhood example of how their system works. He may offer you a number of free items, mention a discount price that you alone will receive, and possibly offer a cash award for each neighbor you send to his company to have the same system installed. He will offer you the company's easy-payment plan if you sign the contract he just happens to have with him.

Even if the company is not outright lar-cenous, you could incur enormous hidden maintenance charges. If replacement parts for the system are not guaranteed available within a specified period of time, you could be without security protection.

The company's payment play may be the standard finance company loan at 18 per-cent, the same used to buy furniture and television sets. However, since you are pay-ing it back through the security company, carrying charges can be added that bring the actual interest rate to 25 percent or more. If you fall behind in the payments, the com-pany can take you to court and try to confis-cate your property.

The company could also be out of busi-ness in a few days. Never sign anything to do with payments or money without first having your lawyer or bank manager go over it with you. If people try to talk you into a quick agreement and urge you to sign with-out delay, there is always something wrong with the deal.

Never rely on anyone who is not recom-mended, locally known, reliable, and well established in business in the area for a long time. This is true, of course, not only for burglar alarms, but for kitchen equipment, siding, roofing, driveways—anything that has to do with your house.

A quick and inexpensive way to secure a double-hung window is to drill holes through the bottom sash into the upper sash and insert a short, snug-fitting nail. An upper sash receptacle can be used to secure the window in an open position, preventing entry, but allowing for ventilation.

LOANS

When you are looking for a loan to finance the security remodeling of your home, the best place to begin is your own bank. Even if they do not make loans of this type, they will be able to advise you on how to get the best loan for your particular needs. Rates, terms, and regulations on loans change, and banks have different lending policies. The amount you are able to borrow will depend on the house, your income, your credit, and what you plan to have done to the house. No reputable financing source will grant you a loan without first seeing a complete set of plans and specifications for the remodeling.

Home Improvement Loan
These loans are sought by most banks be-cause of their high interest yield. Home im-provement loans are nonsecured loans, which means that no liens or debts are placed against the property or the improve-ment unless the loan goes into default. The bank may send a man to inspect your house when you apply, and then again when the remodeling is completed, to see if the money was spent in accordance with your agree-ment. At this writing, the interest rates vary from 9 to 12 percent on a government-guaranteed loan of $10,000, with up to ten years to pay—meaning that if you borrowed $10,000 for ten years at 12 percent, it would cost you $7,215.

Mortgage Loan

If you do not have a mortgage on your home, you may be able to get a straight mortgage from a bank. At the present time, the interest rate is between 8 and 10 percent. The loan or mortgage will depend on the property, the house, what the remodeling entails, and your financial situation. If you do not have a mortgage on the house, it is probably not a good idea to take one out unless the house needs a great deal of work. It is usually better to do what you can step by step and as you can afford it, instead of going into debt.

Mortgage Refinancing

This is an expensive way of financing and you can use it only if you already have a mortgage on your home. You will have to pay off the old mortgage and have a new one drawn up, which involves lawyer's fees, bank charges, and inevitably a higher interest rate than you have been paying.

FHA (Title I) Loan

Next to paying cash, an FHA Title I Home Improvement Loan can be the best way to pay for remodeling. This loan is taken out through a bank. If your income is low and your financial situation is such that no bank wants to lend you money, the Federal Housing Agency can guarantee payment to the bank. The bank can then lend you the money with no risk to itself. Not all banks will handle FHA loans, so you must find one that does. The current maximum you can borrow is $2,500, with an interest rate of 9½ percent.

FHA (K) Loan

A different kind of FHA loan, this is usually suitable for financing more extensive remodeling. These loans are available to those who qualify at 6 percent interest for a minimum of $2,500 and a maximum of $10,000, with twenty years to pay. Fee payments for insurance, service, FHA appraisal and inspections will raise the total cost of the loan slightly. If you are doing any borrowing to finance remodeling, and if you qualify, this is the least expensive loan.

Open-end Mortgage Loan

You must already have a mortgage that permits this type of loan. An open-end mortgage loan provides that you can borrow as much from the bank as you have already paid on your mortgage. Your mortgage is then increased by the amount borrowed, and the length of time the payments are to be made is extended.

Personal Loan

These are loans made by commercial banks at interest rates that currently vary from 12 to 18 percent. The maximum you can borrow is $10,000 for a minimum of three years. These are very expensive and in spite of the high interest rates, excellent credit and references are required.

Finance Company Loan

Almost anyone can get this type of loan, which is usually used to buy automobiles or furniture. These loans should not be used to finance remodeling because the interest rates are very high and vary from 14 to 18 percent on a maximum loan of $2,500. High-pressure home-improvement salesmen carry finance company forms around with them and will try to get you to sign one for work the salesman wants you to let his company do. Never sign one.

Credit Union Loan

A loan from a credit union, if you belong to one, can be a good source of financing to pay for remodeling that is not extensive. Credit union terms and rates are usually very generous, but there is a limit to the amount you can borrow.

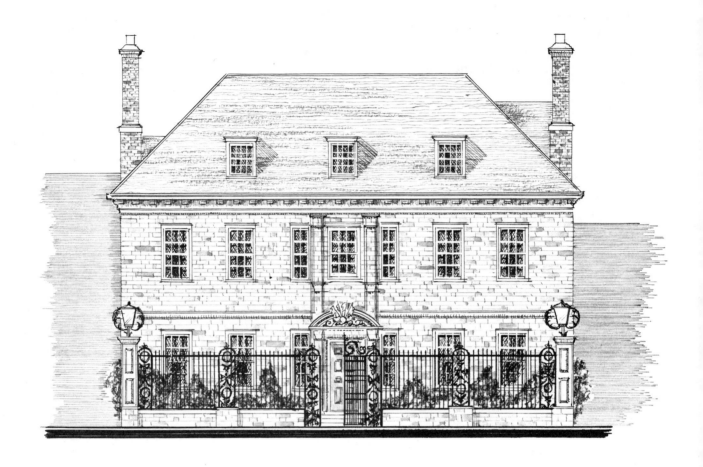

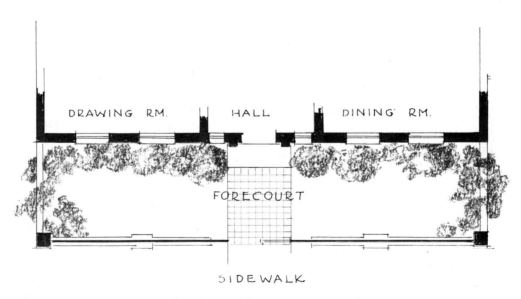

Mompasson House, in Close, Salisbury, was built in 1701 with a forecourt and well-lighted, locked fence protecting the ground floor and entrance. The forecourt is only 12 feet wide by 53 feet long.

Chapter Five

The Landscaping

With the disappearance of the medieval plagues in Europe, more and more people moved into the cultural centers at the beginning of the Renaissance, and the design of cities changed. Because of the more crowded conditions, house plans of the eighteenth century were similar to those of the seventeenth except for two things: they were smaller and provided for more privacy. An increasing amount of stress was laid on convenience in the arrangement of rooms, but the basic living plan, though smaller, remained the same.

A gate opened into a forecourt that was a safe interior space closed off from the street, with stables on one side, kitchen and service areas on the other, and the main two-story residence opposite the entrance gate. Although this may sound quite grand, and in many cases was, depending on the size, the court in some instances was no larger than a modern-day living room, since scale was figured in terms of men and horses.

One of the great contributions of the English to domestic architecture was the residential square. The English townhouse of the eighteenth century was so well planned that the design is still copied today. It had a small forecourt, usually separated from the street by a gate and high fence of wrought iron. The courtyard was planted carefully with a small formal garden. The entrance hall was centered. The dining room, kitchen, and pantry were on the right of the entrance hall, and living and drawing rooms on the left. Bedrooms were upstairs.

The exterior was made of red brick with a slate or tile roof, equally spaced windows, and simple cornices. A small garden was at the rear. These houses were designed in one large unit and were arranged to form a square. For security, the entrance to the square was through a locked gate with a private key for

Overgrown and untrimmed landscaping creates a serious security risk, obscuring doors and windows and shielding prowlers both day and night.

each resident. Some townhouses in Europe have similar arrangements today, but the design has been altered to accommodate that twentieth-century necessity, the automobile. Strong gates are opened and the car enters a roofed area; the gates are closed and the car is driven to a rear courtyard. The driver can leave the car there and enter a walled garden to the house for maximum safety and comfort.

In the United States, of course, we have carried the open lanes and tree-lined streets of our grandfathers' suburbs far into the countryside, making them ineffective for servicing by public transportation or adequate protection by the police. Each house sits with doors and windows staring vacantly at the house across the street, the small yards wasteful of space and water to keep them growing where they lie unused if not unseen.

The landscaping around a house can tell passersby a lot about the owner—his character, his tastes, his income, and what sort of possessions are to be found inside the house. If the grass and landscaping are just about as the builder left them ten years ago, poorly maintained, and with no effort made

The same house with improved landscaping and a widened, safer drive. The overgrown foundation planting has been removed, and the shrubbery set away from the walls to prevent a ground fire from reaching the house.

to hide the garbage cans or pick up a rusted bicycle, the interior of the house will probably reveal the same carelessness. If there is anything worth stealing inside it is probably a large color television and a case of beer.

When the landscaping is spotty, some evergreens here, a few clumps of tired petunias in between protected by little wire fences stuck in the ground, the grass in the back yard worn under the seesaw and around the swings and sandbox—the owner is probably a hardworking man whose wife tends the garden while he tries to keep the grass cut on Saturday afternoon before the ball game.

You know that all of their extra money goes to the orthodontist, the insurance company, and into the savings bank for the kids' education.

Landscaping around the house on all four sides, mixed with shotgun-designed circular flower beds brimming with annuals surrounded by whitewashed rocks and lovingly tended lawn, suggests a retired couple who spend all their time at home. Their most prized possessions will probably be framed photographs of their grandchildren.

A house with flashy, expensive catered landscaping on the front but with none in the

Poorly planted and maintained landscaping and exterior indicate the character of the homeowner.

A busy household with active children leaves little time for anything but superficial landscaping and maintenance.

rear indicates an owner who is more interested in impressing his neighbors than in his home. All his extra money goes into car payments and for trips to Hawaii so he can send postcards to his friends.

Lush, beautifully tended landscape-architect-designed gardens featuring exotic shrubbery and a deep green lawn leading to a swimming pool can be a dead giveaway that the owner lavishes care and money on his property and family, especially if the neighboring homes are not of equal size and similarly maintained. The interior is probably just as luxurious. On the other hand, the owner may just have had to sell the family silver to pay for the pool.

Poorly designed landscaping
can lead to maintenance problems
and create dangerous security problems.

The same house with better,
landscaping and a driveway that does not force
automobiles to back into the street.

Keep the landscaping simple and the foundation trimmed down. Keep shrubbery away from doors and windows and away from the driveway. And do not plant bushes or dig cute little flower beds in the middle of the lawn. They not only make the grass harder to cut but also cast dark shadows at night that give people a place to hide. High foundation planting around windows can give an intruder an opportunity to break or remove glass without being seen. High or dense plantings around doors provides a place to hide, where an intruder can wait for you to come home, mug you, and get inside your house with your own key.

Low planting around the house, uninter-

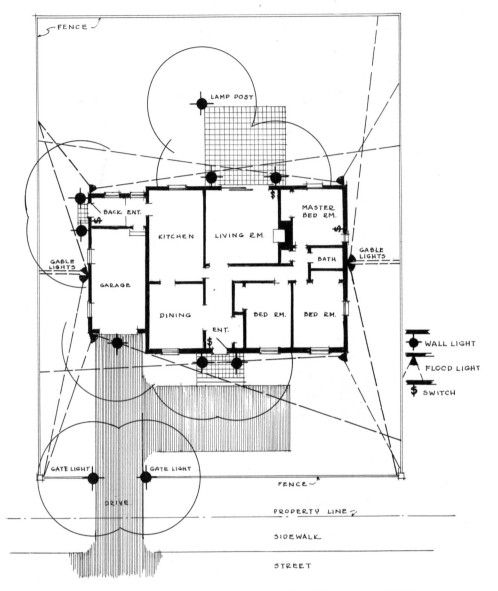

Security lighting should illuminate all doors, walls, and windows. Floodlights mounted high on the corners and gables of the house should be directed on the walls and grounds so that none of the property is thrown into shadow. Switches should be placed beside the front door, back door, and terrace door, and there should be a separate panic switch in the master bedroom to turn on all the lights in case of emergency.

rupted lawns, and lights at night will discourage prowlers. Lighting is important, but if the landscaping is so high or overgrown that it throws areas into shadow, you will be wasting the electricity. Electricity is increasingly expensive, and low-wattage bulbs can accomplish much more with less energy if the trees are kept out of the way. They will

also tend to irritate your neighbors less than bright spotlights shining into their windows.

You should have floodlights on all sides of your house, but these should not be burned all night every night. Not only can they annoy neighbors, because they should be mounted as high on the outside wall as possible, but when you get your electric bill you

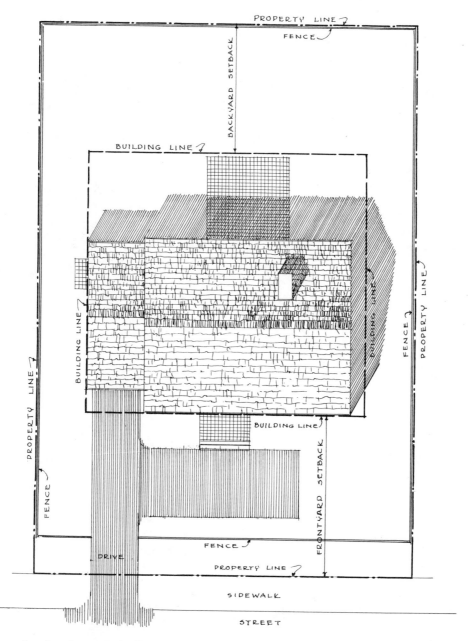

A property survey showing the property lines and permissible building area within. Walls and fences higher than 6 feet must be kept within the building line in most neighborhoods.

may wonder if they were worth it and use them less and less.

A combination of low-wattage lights for continuous use and floodlights for occasional use is best. The low-wattage bulbs should be controlled from the front and back doors, and all floodlights from these locations as well as from the terrace door and the bedroom. Test the floodlighting every two weeks, and let your neighbors know that you are only testing. If they see them burning any other time of the day or night, you should let them know that it means you are in trouble. Robberies take place in the daytime, too, or you could need help for some other reason.

PICKET

SPLIT RAIL

LATTICE

POST AND BOARD

Four of the most common "candy-box" types of fences, serving only to mark the property lines. Easily sealed, they are no deterrent to an intruder.

STOCKADE

LOUVER

BOARD AND BATTEN

CHAIN LINK

These fences, built to a height of 8 feet, will help discourage all but the most determined prowler. A fence this high will become part of the architecture, and serious consideration should be given to a design that will complement the house.

A traditional picket fence can be made more secure by building it higher on a brick or masonry foundation that cannot be dug under. For further protection, it can be topped with inconspicuous strands of barbed wire.

THE FENCE

Fences, regardless of how low, define the exact extent of your property so that it cannot be mistaken by anyone—you, the police, or a prowler. Someone on the outside of the fence is just looking, someone on the inside is trespassing. Mark your property lines with a fence, the higher the better. Just how high will depend on zoning laws. The material the fence is made of will depend on your neighbors and the police protection you have.

Zoning ordinances permit fences and walls within the permissible building area of the site to be as high as the house walls. Outside the building area, they can limit the height of the fence or wall to four or sometimes three feet. This is done for better fire and police protection so the property can be surveyed from an automobile. The height of hedges is usually not regulated except at street intersections, to provide drivers with a clear view of the oncoming traffic.

The police prefer being able to see over and through fences and, in areas where the police are able to patrol constantly, this visibility may be a safeguard. However, not in all sections of the country and not in all cities can the already overburdened police manage this. In some cities the police can answer a call reporting a breaking and entering within three minutes. In other, high-crime areas it can take up to an hour for the police to answer a call. This will make a difference in how high you want your fence to be and of what material you want it built.

If you know your neighbors well and they are not constantly away, you may want to use a chain-link fence they can see through, even climb over in case of trouble. If you live in an area constantly harassed by drug addicts, drunks, muggings, with a lot of juvenile attacks on the elderly and without adequate police protection, you may want a concrete wall eight feet high around your property if zoning will permit it.

Concrete and concrete block are fireproof and require no maintenance. Concrete structures must be built on a foundation wall three feet below grade in most parts of the country, thereby discouraging people from digging under the wall; but this makes them very expensive to build, and if their height is restricted by zoning ordinances so that they provide little more than a visible obstruction without real protection, their cost is usually not warranted. Solid walls of masonry can also keep out breezes, a disadvantage in summer and in warm climates.

A chain-link fence can be reinforced with masonry supports and softened with climbing roses. Metal fences can be electrified for additional security, but this may not be permitted in some locations.

A wire fence can be taken below the ground to prevent digging under. If electrifying or topping with barbed wire is not permitted a good stand of climbing roses can be just as effective, and no one is going to outlaw roses.

Solid or open walls of bricks can be laid economically one brick wide if the wall is laid in a serpentine manner, adding stiffness to the wall instead of bulk. Few communities have large enough building sites to allow for this kind of brick construction, and conventional brick courses will have to be laid, their thickness depending on the height.

Wood walls and fences can burn; most require some form of maintenance and do not equal the security standards of masonry. The kind of fence you choose will largely depend on what you want it to do and the

architectural design of your house. You would not want to use a stockade or a split-rail fence with a house of formal Georgian architecture or a sophisticated plywood or louvered fence with a Cape Cod house.

Sufficiently high stockade fences can give you fairly good security if they are sturdily built and the sections are bolted together. They allow a little of the breeze through, but are difficult to look through unless pried apart; they will keep stray cats and dogs off the property.

Picket, lattice, slat, louver, and split-rail fences are the candy-box type of fence used to define the edge of the property and to allow air and vision through it. They are seldom high enough or strong enough to be considered for their security value. They do have decorative possibilities and, when covered with roses or pyracantha, offer a certain limited resistance to an intruder if they are designed for the purpose.

Board-on-board and board-and-batten fences offer more privacy and additional security, but they are made of wood that, unless it is redwood, has to be preserved with stain or paint. Because of the amount of wood and paint required, if these fences are to be sturdy and high enough to offer any security, they are expensive to build and maintain.

For security, for a breeze, and to allow the police department to have surveillance of the property, metal chain-link fences are usually considered the best protection for large estates and industrial use. Taken to a height of seven feet or more, they can be topped with barbed wire for additional protection. They are steel, expensive, and very discouraging to prowlers if properly constructed. Their only drawback is that they are ugly. But they work. Consequently, more people are using them and try to obscure their commercial aspects with ivy, shrubbery and trees. Unfortunately, this can be detrimental to their use as secure fencing.

Corrugated metal, fiberglass, plastic, or solid plywood combined with translucent panels can make an attractive and safe fence when taken below grade.

THE GATE

The most vulnerable part of a fence is usually the gate. Because of the reinforcement needed to allow it to swing without sagging, intruders can climb over it if they cannot go through it.

Even if the fence is for decorative purposes and to define the property line, you should have a gate. Few people will climb over a fence when they can walk through an opening in it, and you can have the gate wired to ring in the house and notify you if the gate is opened. Even if it is not a burglar, the warning can give you enough time to pick up the Sunday papers before your relatives arrive for a surprise visit. It will also let you keep tabs on the children if they are not supposed to leave the yard.

Light the driveway gate on each side and keep the shrubbery away from it. The gate should be at least 18 feet back from the street to allow you to pull your car completely onto your own property before you open the gate. This way the front of the car will not be sticking out on the highway when you get out of it to close the gate as you leave.

Avoid the temptation to make the gate so ornamental that it looks like the entrance to Woodlawn Cemetery. Do not have your name on the gate or on the outside of your house regardless of how proud you are of either. If you have a rural delivery mailbox in front of your house, print only the box number, not your name, on it. The mailman will not forget you. Crooks will not either. If they see in the paper that your family is having a wedding, funeral, or vacation trip, they can confirm that the house is empty and break in and rob you while you are out.

Gates in low fences can be effective if properly secured. Walkway gates should be lighted and wired to sound a buzzer in the house when opened.

Driveway gates should be locked and lighted from both sides. A locked driveway gate, even on a low fence, can prevent someone from driving in with a car or van to haul stolen goods away.

A sturdy plank gate in a high concrete block wall. Openings in the alternate layers of plank allow air circulation and a view of the drive and garage. Three-way lights in the wall illuminate both sides of the wall and the gate.

A cardinal door, as used in massive charch doors, allows pedestrians to enter without opening up the entire door. Heavy wire attached diagonally with a turnbuckle will brace a sagging gate.

Driveway gates can make a strong statement in these otherwise nondescript metal fences of chain link and heavy wire.

A 9-foot-wide drive is adequate for a garage at the rear of the lot. The spaces indicated are the minimum required for backing and turning out of a garage or parking space in one turn.

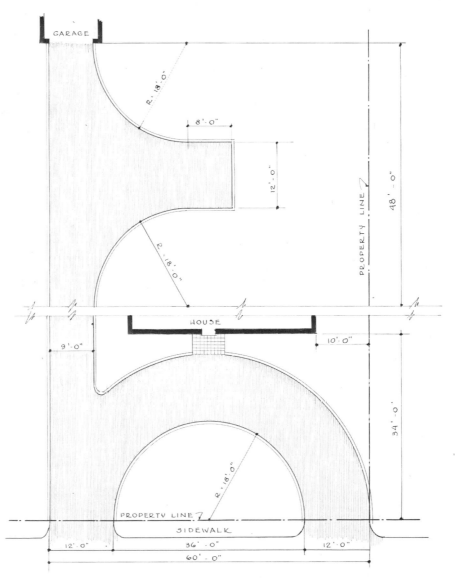

A safe circular drive is possible on a lot width as small as 60 feet, using minimum dimensions based on a turning radius of 19 feet required for a Chevrolet. A Cadillac 75 limousine would require a turning radius of 27 feet.

The minimum area required for the average American car in backing out of a garage and driving forward into the street in two turns.

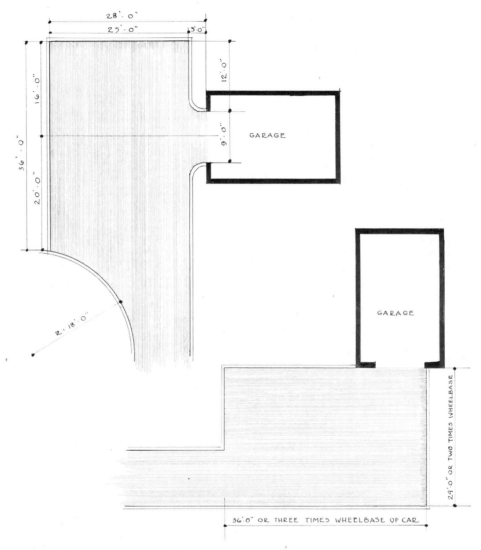

The minimum space required for backing out of a garage and driving forward into the street in three turns.

THE DRIVEWAY

When you drive home at night, the lights of your car should illuminate the front door and, if possible, the back door as well. It is too easy for a prowler to hang around the front door and, if spotted, act confused, a little drunk, and ask, "Isn't this the Jones house?" If anything looks disturbed when you arrive home at night, drive on. Call the police from another telephone, and let them go to the house and check it. If you find a strange truck or van in your driveway at any

time, day or night, drive on and get help.

A house with a driveway that does not go past the front door has no front door. It only has an inconvenient entrance. Smaller cars and smaller turning radiuses on cars allow all but the smallest lots to have a circular drive that goes past the front door and does not force you to back into the street.

Even a large Cadillac, which has a turning radius of only 30 feet, can make a U turn in 60 feet, an Oldsmobile in about 50 feet, and a Jeep in slightly under 38 feet. Lots as narrow as 30 feet can still have driveways designed

A dangerous unlighted garage surrounded by close trees that can conceal a mugger or prowler. Even when the garage doors are closed, windows in the overhead door reveal whether a car is in the garage of if the family is away from the property.

for them that do not require backing out into the street.

THE GARAGE

The first thing to remember about the garage is the door. Keep it closed and locked all the time. Not only will a closed garage door not indicate to strangers whether you are home or not, it is safer even when you are home.

Besides, there is nothing quite so unattractive as a garage door gaping open, like a mouth without teeth. If the garage is detached from the house, you may not need an automatic door since you will have to brave the weather getting into the house anyway. But make sure the doors are well lighted and that there is no shrubbery around where someone can hide so that, while you are opening the garage door, he can get into your car and drive off with it. An open garage door invites someone either into the

The same garage can be made safe by removing overgrown trees and installing an automatic door. A walled or fenced walkway, shown here as a chain-link fence, provides safe passage from garage to house.

house or, even worse, into the garage to wait for you to return.

Have switches for the light on the path from the garage to the back door of the house both in the garage and inside the back door so the lights can be turned on and off from either location. Do not store ladders in the garage, making it easy for a prowler to use your own ladder to climb in an upper-floor window at the back of the house.

If the garage is attached to or part of the house, have an automatic garage door.

Each time you drive into the garage, look at the door connecting the garage to the house. If this door looks tampered with, back out immediately and get help. Hopefully you will not have a lot of items stored in the garage that could conceal a person and you will have been driving with the car doors locked so you cannot be taken by surprise. If something looks tampered with, never get out of the car in the garage to investigate. Get help from the police before entering the house.

An unlighted, tree-shrouded terrace can be an invitation to a prowler, who can hide behind shrubbery. Heavy vines on a stout trellis can be used as a ladder to second-floor windows.

THE TERRACE

Terraces are a part of the house and the garden because they are used for the outdoor living we love so much. However, insofar as security is concerned, terraces should be considered part of the lawn, part of the no-man's-land between the edge of your property and the house, part of the property that should be lighted at night with no shadows or surrounding trees or shrubbery to hide someone who does not belong there.

Since terrace doors are a constant attraction to a prowler, they should always be carefully locked, lighted, and illuminated by floodlights in case of emergency.

Taking all the precautions will, of course, destroy some of the privacy of the terrace. It can be screened from the street and neighbors only with the use of fences or

With the property fenced in and better landscaping and lighting designed, the terrace is safer. The stairs to the sliding glass doors have been remodeled to eliminate hiding places and to make quick escape and removal of stolen property more difficult.

walls, and we must consider whether that privacy is valuable enough to sacrifice the security of the house.

If walls or fences are used, they should be high enough and strong enough to discourage any prowler. Fencing should be used only at the property lines and privacy planting on the terrace side of the fence eliminated, with unbroken open lawns between fence and terrace.

Terraces can sometimes be partially enclosed by the addition of a garage or garden house, but these, like walls, are governed by the zoning ordinances. The old-fashioned open terrace, surrounded by landscaping and secluded by trees under the stars, is rapidly becoming only a fond memory because it is simply too dangerous to be used in most neighborhoods. Check local zoning and plan your terrace for maximum security.

THE LANDSCAPING | 79

Using concepts from the past, a modern chain-link fence permits visibility of house and driveway and at the same time secures the doors and windows. Additional security can be given bedroom or basement windows by fencing in an extended light well.

A Roman house, typical of those built around courtyards for security and privacy. A small shop, on the left, could be run by the owner or rented out. The shop entrance, like all openings to the street, was secured at night with a heavy wooden panel.

Chapter Six

Courtyards

The streets of a typical Roman town were probably just as busy as Wall Street at noon on any Wednesday—noisy, dusty, crowded, and bustling. They were probably almost as bad at night, when Roman law decreed that all deliveries had to be made so citizens would not be endangered dodging loaded carts. But the Romans had the good sense to build their houses around a courtyard and turn their backs on the public streets. They had an extensive water supply and sewer system and paved streets, and the precious secure land within the city walls was not wasted on unproductive patches of space we call front, back, and side yards.

The house wall started at the building line on the street. The courtyard was the center of the house and provided a safe, cool, quiet retreat from the sometimes dangerous streets on the other side of the front door, which was usually the only entrance and was kept closed and locked at all times. There were no windows on the street, or if there were, they were small openings high in the wall and on upper floors of the house in unimportant rooms. All were barred and shuttered at night. For light and ventilation all doors and windows opened to the courtyard.

In North America—not so much in South America, where they have inherited Spanish design—this conception has been completely turned around. In the suburbs especially, houses used to be built with a big front porch for socializing and outdoor living. There was a back porch for the cook and utilities, such as the laundry tubs and the icebox. It used to be pleasant on a summer evening to sit on the front porch in the wicker furniture with a glass of iced tea, wave to friends as they strolled by, and see who got off the trolley down by the corner. Now

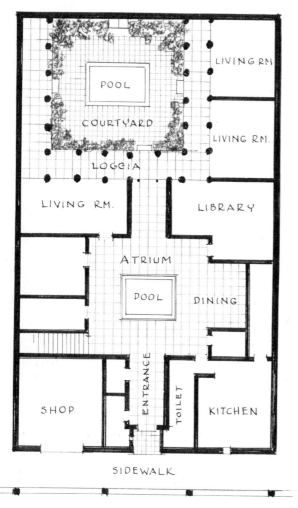

POOL

COURTYARD

LOGGIA

LIVING RM

LIVING RM.

LIVING RM.

LIBRARY

ATRIUM

POOL

DINING

SHOP

ENTRANCE

TOILET

KITCHEN

SIDEWALK

STREET

The courtyard of the Roman house shown here and on page 82 was a safe and quiet retreat away from the street. Most of the activity took place in the atrium, lighted by an opening in the roof, which also allowed light and air into the upstairs bedrooms.

A. J. Harmon

Gone are the spacious front porches and broad lawns of our grandmothers' day, where the family could sit in the shade and spend the evening nodding to their friends as they strolled past.

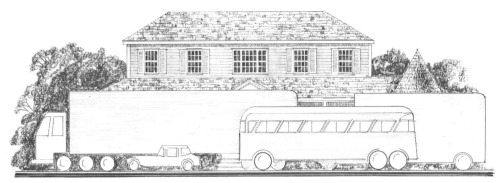

Strolling pedestrians, trolley cars, and horses have given way to noisy, air-polluting traffic, making the porch an outdated, dangerous, and wasteful expense.

if you tried that, your iced tea would get dirty, you could be overcome by gasoline fumes, and take a chance on being mugged or of having your house robbed by the back door while you sat in front. The front porch was a charming and characteristically American space back in the days when we were safe from our neighbors, when people still actually lived in houses on Main Street within walking distance of a safe park, when children walked to the same high school their parents had attended.

After the automobile brought an end to the front porch, it became the thing to have a terrace or a porch out back to get away from the noise and dirt of the traffic. Since nobody could afford a cook, the space was wasted anyway. Then everybody moved inside to watch television, and the suburban crime rate rose until it became too dangerous to be outside at night where it was cool in the summer. Air-conditioning was a big thing there for a while, but an energy crisis was declared, electricity rates skyrocketed,

An average-sized man (5 feet, 10 inches) can easily see and climb over a 4-foot high wall.

Even a 6-foot-high wall can easily be scaled, since the average man can reach 7 feet, 5½ inches without jumping.

Hedges planted on the inside of a 4-foot wall allow easy access over an 8-foot-high privet simply by one's standing on top of the wall.

A hedge planted on the outside of the wall prevents access. Hedges fortified with barbed or electrified wire will discourage pushing through the hedge.

and most people were reluctant to run their machines to cool off their houses.

After two thousand years we are just about back where we started—living behind walls. Without walls there are no courtyards, and without walls there are few places to relax securely outdoors at night. On the other hand, you may not be permitted to have the walls either. That will depend on the zoning ordinances and the zoning board governing your property.

Many houses, especially those built in de-

velopments, are constructed right up to the permissible building line, and before you can erect a wall or fence higher than the predetermined height, you have to apply for a variance in the zoning ordinance. A variance may or may not be granted. If it is not, and you are limited to enclosing your property to a height of four feet, do not plan on a secure outdoor living area. A height of four feet is only enough to keep out stray dogs and cats.

Even a six-foot-high masonry wall, while it will serve as a deterrent, will only be ex-

An L-shaped house lends itself to the creation of a courtyard, providing security and privacy.

BEFORE

AFTER

This 8-foot wall, made with plastic-coated chain link stretched between heavy wood supports, allows for breeze and visibility. Climbing roses on the wall and used as a ground cover discourage close approach to or scaling of the chain link.

pensive and create a false sense of security. A wall this high is easily scaled and can invite the curious to see what is on the other side. This is not difficult to understand when you consider that a standard door height is six feet eight inches.

You can add additional height and protection by planting a privet hedge on the outside of the wall if you do not have to walk on your neighbor's property to trim it. The height of the hedge is unlimited by ordinances in most cases, but it will not offer

any protection planted on the inside of the wall, and to get a tall dense growth the hedge must be trimmed from both sides and the top. This can take years.

Using a seven- or eight-foot-high chain-link fence with barbed wire on top of it or a similar masonry or wood wall to create a courtyard will give you reasonably comfortable security. (I use the term "courtyard" loosely here, for a true courtyard should be surrounded on three sides by the house.) It will take effort and equipment to get through

A solid-board-and-batten wall built over a stone planter creates a quiet, safe courtyard further protected by thorny roses. Several strands of electrified barbed wire hidden in the roses would provide additional security along walls next to a driveway, where entrance over the wall could be accomplished from the roof of a truck or van.

or over such a wall—a ladder, a crowbar, or a saw. And it will certainly discourage someone who just happens to be passing from breaking in.

Walls will not stop professional burglars—after all, they break out of jail, so why not into your home?—although they will probably come through the door, not over a wall. But these are not people you can worry about, and unless they are crazier than most, they will not break in when they know you are there. They are out to rob you

quietly, not to meet you or hurt you.

The people you want to protect yourself from are the ones that want what you have at any cost and are desperate and reckless or insane enough to do anything to get it. You also need to protect yourself and your property from wanton acts of vandalism created by the mobile youth who can catch sight of a clean, comfortable room through a window and decide to wreck it. If courtyard walls conceal the contents of your house, these and the desperate are less likely to act rashly

An entrance court can provide protection for prominent ground-floor rooms, improving the value and often the appearance of the house. The gate can be hinged or can slide on barn-door hardware. Children and pets can play safely behind the wall, and electrical devices can be used to detect intruders or notify residents of visitors.

on impulse after a quick look through the sliding glass terrace doors.

Courtyard walls eight feet high allow you the freedom of being able to leave doors and windows facing them open during the day and early evening without risking a chance inspection of your furnishings, television sets, paintings, and even your living habits. This is why solid walls, while in some instances perhaps not as secure as chain-link fencing topped with barbed wire, are better. They cannot be looked through or cut.

Courtyards are not limited to the back of your house. One in front can make your front door more secure, screen windows of important rooms facing the street, and perhaps even allow you to walk from the garage to the door in relative security. However, the wall must be at least eight feet high or more and, ideally, devoid of planting.

In the Orient, street after street in the residential neighborhoods presents a public facade of gray, lifeless walls and sturdy but unimpressive and almost identical gates.

Walls along a typical Japanese street protect the grounds of the most humble houses or elegant mansions without revealing what is beyond the traditional gate.

Anyone could be living behind the wall, from a respectable but poor carpenter to the wealthiest merchant prince. Once inside the walls, however, the carpenter's sparse house is open to a small but lovely garden he carefully tends, and beyond the prince's gate next door may lie a priceless seventeenth-century forty-room mansion surrounded by lavish gardens and pools, separate servants' quarters, stables, and a fifteen-car garage for his collection of Rolls-Royces.

When these homes are robbed the thieves are usually caught, because it is an inside job. Only a well-informed crook would know which wall to climb over. It is even difficult to find a house by its number, because the houses are numbered in the order in which they were built, not by their order on the street.

Courtyards usually connect various areas of the same house or two or more structures on the same site. If, for instance, you have a detached garage and do not like crossing the

Even the smallest Japanese house will have a private courtyard surrounded by the main rooms of the house. A narrow exterior passage can be used as a porch or closed off by sliding glass or paper shoji to become part of the room.

yard or driveway to get to the house, consider connecting the two with walls, creating a secure outdoor living area between them. While it will not be exactly a courtyard, you will have a secure way to get from your car into the house and at the same time a place where you can relax in the evening in privacy and security.

Remember, however, when measuring areas outdoors and laying them out with string, they will look very small staked out. This can lead to some startling results after the walls have been built and the area seems three or four times as large as you expected.

Treat any courtyard as an outdoor room

much like a living room, dining room, or kitchen. Know how you are going to use it and what function it is to serve. If the courtyard connects any two buildings on the site, such as the house and the garage, roof over a passage between them to keep the snow and rain off as you pass back and forth. This does add to the cost, but it allows the courtyard to function on various levels—first as security, and second as added living space.

There is no reason not to consider an outdoor grill for cooking over charcoal. While grills are too dangerous indoors because of the fumes produced by charcoal, a courtyard is a perfect place for cooking and dining

A dining courtyard connecting the garage to the house can be an excellent place to relax and entertain. A charcoal grill built in the connecting passage is the focal point for an outdoor kitchen protected from the weather. Flowers, vegetables, and herbs can be grown just outside the kitchen door.

out. You will not have to worry about the neighbors or their pets dropping in, and if one side of the courtyard is protected by a covered passage you will not have to worry about rain upsetting your dinner. The passage can also provide a good place to store furniture out of the rain.

Solid courtyard walls will keep the wind off the courtyard and let you use it early in the spring and late in the fall. Courtyards can even be used in the dead of winter if you have the grill under the roofed area. Pipes filled with antifreeze set in the masonry floor of the courtyard and running around the fire pit of the grill will melt the snow and ice and

can provide a bit of warmth from the floor and the fire itself on a windless winter night.

The courtyard walls do not have to be solid, and if you live in the southern part of the country you may not want solid walls that radiate heat and keep away the breeze. However, trellised concrete blocks made for this purpose or trellised wooden walls can act as built-in ladders and offer almost none of the security of a solid wall. They should be considered only as a privacy screen that can conceal an intruder working away undetected on doors and windows.

If you must use open concrete blocks for ventilation on a small courtyard, place them

A board-and-batten garden house and court entrance, ventilated with a cupola to avoid the use of windows on outside walls. All courtyard entrances should be as secure as the house doors.

only in the lowest second or third course of blocks. This will allow cooler air next to the ground to circulate and not permit the openings to be used as ladder rungs for someone to climb.

Certainly masonry topped with several lines of barbed wire is the most secure wall since it is difficult to climb over, is fireproof, and cannot be seen through. The wire at the top can also be connected to an alarm that will go off if a ladder is leaned against it, if it is cut or otherwise interfered with by anything except a resting bird. It can also be wired to produce an electric shock.

In some areas with diligent police protection, large sections of chain-link fence interspersed with the masonry would permit a breeze, and the police could see through if they were looking—but so could anyone else. An enclosure entirely made of chain-link fence is not a courtyard so much as a fenced yard, although in time, with vines and privet, it could be made to seem like a courtyard.

Wooden courtyard walls can be compatible with some architectural styles, but like chain-link fencing, unless given a continuous footing, they can be dug under; they are

A half-timber garden house and courtyard wall made of old railroad ties. The spaces between the ties can be filled with stone and brick rubble and plastered, or prestuccoed plywood panels can be used.

not fireproof, need maintenance, and in the long run cost more money than masonry. Wood must also be braced every twelve to sixteen feet unless masonry supports are used. This is not true of house walls because interior partitions and the floor and roof joist brace the walls. Outdoors, with nothing covering or bracing the walls, weather and wind can soon batter them, making them dangerous as security protection.

The average homeowner has an advantage building the courtyard walls out of blocks himself because, while not easy work, it is relatively simple if you go slowly and follow a few basic rules of house construction.

If you have a garden house within the courtyard on an outside wall, it can be used as a gatehouse as well as for storage. When the courtyard must be built within the building lines there is property at the back and sides that needs attention, and a garden house can be used to service both so that equipment and plants for the courtyard do not need to be brought through the house.

The door to the garden house should be just as well locked and protected as the front door of the house. Any windows in the garden house should face the courtyard unless

The circle has particular significance in the Orient. Here it is used as an entrance to a courtyard hundreds of years old in the Yunan province of southwest China. A modern variation could be made with a sliding wooden door mounted with barn-door hardware.

they are high, barred, and used for ventilation only. If additional ventilation is needed in the garden house, as it might be where tools, fertilizer, and other things are stored, a cupola on the roof is serviceable and can be very attractive.

A gate into the courtyard is often necessary for maintenance and should be as secure as any door into the house. The gate should open in so there is no chance of anyone's being able to tamper with or remove the hinges. This will mean that if it is not a strong gate it can also be pushed in, so the same procedure should be followed for securing it as for the front door, but you can further secure the gate by dropping a plank across it, held in place by metal clamps. Light it as you would the house doors, and include a peep hole so you can see who is there before you open it.

This carriage gate into a courtyard leading from the street to a loggia is typical of those in New Orleans on Church Street or Legare Street, built in the eighteenth century.

If you have alarms on other doors and windows, the courtyard gate should also have one. When alarms are not used on other doors, a motion-sensitive bell can be placed on the gate, similar to those used by shopkeepers to alert them when a customer enters the store. The gate can also be wired to sound an alarm bell in the house when it is opened.

A pressure-sensitive mat can be placed on the exterior of the gate to sound a buzzer in the house if it is approached.

Light both the interior and the exterior of the courtyard walls as you would the house walls, with low-wattage lights for illumination at night and with floodlights for an emergency. Connect the lights to the same switches used for the house wall lights. Light the entrance gate to the courtyard as you would a door into the house.

A secure modern courtyard with pool and a screened living area in a small forest of bamboo. Living-room and bedroom windows (and even basement windows if they are set in a wide, deep lightwell) can safely be left open for ventilation.

A. J. Harmon

The cliff dwellings of the Pueblo Indians were built for protection, with the roofs used for circulation, living, and recreation as in this town of Betatakin.

Chapter Seven

Roof Gardens

The Egyptians may not have been the first to use their roofs as living spaces, but they did refine the use of roofs in a grand manner. It rained very little in Egypt, and they did not have to concern themselves with extensive waterproofing of the flat roofs, made from sun-baked mud bricks or from stone excavated from the extensive quarries lining the Nile. The entire commerce of Egypt depended on the river, which overflowed its banks every year between July and October, depositing fertile topsoil in the Nile Valley on both sides of the river. Just beyond this narrow valley there was nothing for miles but rock cliffs and desert. Good land was scarce, and while there existed the vast palaces of the pharaohs, the average Egyptian citizen built up instead of out, and homes of two or more stories with a loggia on top were common.

Thick walls and roofs protected the houses from the intense heat and brilliance of the sun during the hot days. Windows, if there were any at all, were often no more than mere slits, so that only a minimum of sun could enter during the day. At night when the sun went down and cool breezes swept across the valley from the desert, the Egyptians gathered their skirts around them and went up to the cool roofs for the evening. Not only did the higher elevation of the roof put them in a better location to catch the breeze, it got them up and away from the heat and dust of the street and away from the cooking odors of the kitchens. They were also more secure, seeing what was happening on the streets below without having to be part of it; probably, however, security was a second consideration to them and they were more concerned with comfort. Thousands of years after the Egyptians built up for comfort, the tower house evolved in Europe, and houses were built up for reasons of security.

An Egyptian house with front and rear courtyards and the all-important roof garden. Shade for the roof is provided here by a formal loggia, although often simple mats on wood poles were used.

A. A. Harmon

In Pueblo villages such as this one, called Acoma, in New Mexico, a lookout could spot strangers miles away from the rooftops. At night the ladders were hauled up for security.

We waste our roofs, and what more delightful and secure part of the house and garden is there, surrounded by living green leaves? Remember the tree house you had or wanted as a child, and the secure feeling of peace in the leaves after the rope ladder was pulled up?

Flat roofs cost more to build than pitched roofs finished off with shingles. Even to design a house with a flat roof is more difficult than to do one with a pitched roof. Just look around—how many attractive flat-roofed houses are there?

Flat roofs require drainage, a four-ply waterproof membrane roof, plus a finish that can withstand furniture legs and traffic. Unless your present roof and roof structure need to be replaced, you are probably not going to level it to add a new flat roof; in existing houses this can be prohibitive. Property restrictions, either in the deed or in a zoning ordinance, may not permit flat roofs to be built covering the entire house in your area. However, if you are adding space to your house, you will want to consider roofing it with a flat roof that can be used as

A flat-roofed house, which lends itself to a roof garden, before and after remodeling. Interior stairs have been added, along with a loggia and penthouse, which can be used to store roof-garden furniture and double as a greenhouse in winter. The picture window has been blocked off to conserve fuel and insure privacy. In summer the shutters on first-floor windows are closed, and warm air is drawn off through the open doors of the penthouse.

This flat roof, remodeled into a protected roof garden, has ample room for an arbor, penthouse, and interior stair. A solid railing on the right blocks off a view and noise from the street. An open railing on the left allows the breeze to circulate.

a roof garden. If your house already has a flat roof, by all means get it in shape to be used after checking to be sure it is structurally sound and capable of handling the added weight of people, plants, and furniture.

Outdoor living space on the roof that can be reached only through the house can be a very dramatic and exciting experience. A roof garden can also have a loggia over part of it to house the stairs, provide shade, and make storage available for furniture, flower pots, and gardening equipment. An inexpensive plastic cold water hose bib can be carried to the roof to make watering and cleaning easier.

A closed railing will give you more privacy, and, because of that, more security than a standard-height open railing, usually 32 to 36 inches high, depending on your local building code. If you have a view you want to see, make sure you establish the railing height from a sitting position so the horizon-

A high louvered wall around this roof garden blocks off neighborhood sights and sounds but lets the breeze through. Selected views can be had by using ventilating shutters in various openings. Sliding glass doors with grilles dividing them prevent anyone from walking into the glass.

tal handrail does not cut it in half or block it.

Higher, solid railings will cut down on the ventilation if that is a serious consideration on the roof garden. It usually is not because the roof is exposed, but if it is you can use louvered shutters for the railing to control the ventilation.

For additional security on a roof garden, carry the railing higher in the form of a wall eight feet high or more. If this creates ventilation problems, you can use standard house windows down in the wall, protected by shutters or an iron grille. You could also simply use a grille in the openings and cover them with shutters or let vines grow over them for privacy where it is needed.

The roof can be screened for insect control or the roof area covered with heavy wire mesh for tighter security and to prevent access from the top. Heavy wire will also support grape vines, tomato plants, or other vegetables and vines for shade.

A loggia built of wood and wire to support vines for shade on a roof garden with a built-in bench. A low railing that does not hide the view is made safe with the addition of an upper screened section. The top of the bench is hinged to store seat covers in bad weather.

Both the walls and the roof area of a roof garden can be made of heavy wire or chain link if it is to be used for tennis, badminton, or some other sport, providing security and ventilation. Care will need to be taken with the design to provide for privacy, but this can usually be handled with screens or vines.

Heavy plant boxes and planters should be placed on the perimeter of the roof over lower supporting walls. While they may not weigh an excessive amount when they are first planted, the additional weight of the grown plants and of the water used to keep them growing could overload the roof structure. However, if planters are placed over

A privacy and security screen of chain link protects this roof garden. Covered with vines, areas of the chain link are removed to provide selected views and to prevent vines from blocking off air circulation.

Heavy planters should be confined to the exterior circumference of the roof garden over the structural walls of the house. Light and ventilation for an interior room or hallway below the roof garden is provided by a clerestory cupola, which can also be used for seating or sun-bathing.

structural walls, not partitions in the center of the roof, and are not huge, you are not likely to overload the structure. Big, deep planters or unusual design concepts should always be checked with an architect or engineer to be sure there will be no unexpected stress placed on the roof and the supporting walls.

In northern climates the flowers and vines will have to be replaced every year because the roots will freeze in the shallow plant boxes. Vines growing from the ground up a wall or trellis will not have to be replaced because they will not freeze out, but they can be an open invitation for someone to climb them to get to the roof garden.

Even the roof of a small penthouse stair can be used for sun-bathing, relaxing, or as a secret hideaway for children when the roof garden is being used by adults. Here the railings serve as planters.

A screened roof garden with deep planters containing mature trees. In the center is a small reflecting pool and fountain with seating surrounding it. The screen roof is slanted at a steep angle to prevent leaves from settling on it. Heavy planters, pools, and furniture require a special structure, which should be designed by an engineer.

In southern climates, the plants will do well all year if fertilized and watered. The plants and the additional roof thickness plus the cooling process of evaporating water will help keep rooms under a roof garden cooler in the summer and will thus lower air-conditioning costs.

A flat roof is not perfectly flat. It should be slightly pitched for drainage so water and snow will not build up, adding to the weight on the roof. Usually a slope of 1/8 inch to 1/4 inch to the foot is all that is required and the surface of the roof will still appear to be flat. Flat roofs will not leak if they are properly

An Oriental roof garden with built-in furniture and perimeter planters. Canvas- or plastic-covered shoji slide over the circular opening for privacy, or can be slid away completely for maximum air circulation on all three sides of the roof garden.

Lightweight, inexpensive duckboards and built-in benches on different levels create an interesting roof garden for private sun-bathing. The canvas pillows can be stored in the hinged bench during the winter, and hung on the wall where they will dry quickly after a summer rain.

constructed and waterproofed. Structural members, the joists, must be much heavier than those on a pitched roof, where the weight of wind and snow is taken by the rafters and not the horizontal joists. Often the joists in a flat roof will have to be placed closer together than the usual 16 inches on center used on pitched roofs. Bridging should be used between all the joists.

Because a standard four- or five-ply built-up roof, made with alternate layers of felt and tar, cannot be walked on, a finished walking surface must be applied over the waterproofing. When the roof is not going to be used for recreation and living space, it is usually protected from weathering and occasional foot traffic for servicing by a layer of gravel. Gravel is not suitable for an actively used surface such as a roof garden because the traffic can wear holes and otherwise damage the waterproof membrane or the plies of tar and felt underneath.

Wood, in the form of removable duckboards—individual platforms nailed together on two-by-fours with spaces between the boards to allow water to drain off—fitted to the top of the roof in sections, can be used to protect the roof surface. Duckboards are probably the lightest-weight protection you can use over the floor of the roof garden, but they are not fireproof and will have to be replaced from time to time and kept stained or painted.

Quarry tile is an excellent fireproof and weatherproof floor for a roof garden, but if it is to be used, its weight should be provided for when the roof is being designed because it can weigh from five to six pounds per square foot if it is a half inch thick.

Thinly cut slate as well as cut brick can also be used for the floor of the roof garden. Any material that is used, if not conventional, should be first checked by an engineer to be sure it can accomplish what it is supposed to do.

This tiled bathing and roof garden is built on a number of levels around a large hot tub or pool with shower. Shuttered openings on pool level adjust for breeze or privacy.

An inexpensive roof garden and greenhouse using one wall of the penthouse to supply water and heat. Vents at the top of the greenhouse prevent heat from building up in summer and also draw off warm air from the house below.

Some recent developments in plywood have produced a lightweight plywood sheet, finished with a weatherproof, nonslip surface, that can be used as a roof-garden floor. Some manufacturers claim that they have developed a plastic-based paint that will waterproof exterior-grade plywood so that it can be used as a terrace surface, but these should all be investigated before they are used, and they must be guaranteed.

In many cases a flat roof would not be compatible with the design of the house, but many houses already have flat roofs that are being wasted and could be put to good use.

BEFORE

AFTER

The addition of a bedroom or bathroom provides an excellent opportunity to include a roof garden. Stair and access can be provided through a penthouse or, as here, by an inexpensive shed dormer.

In houses where an addition of a bedroom or even something as small as a bathroom is being planned, it can be roofed with a flat roof that is suitable to the design of the house.

The roof garden does not have to be extensive to be enjoyable. Rather than spend a lot of money building and securing a ground-floor terrace, it might be much better to invest in a small roof garden that could be used much like an old-fashioned sleeping porch on hot nights. If this is the intent, you will want higher solid railings and parapets, not only for security but for privacy.

A detached fireproof concrete-block garage includes a roof garden reached from the entrance hall by a circular stair and bridge. The bridge also provides cover from the garage to the house. Additional security is provided by an entrance courtyard.

A. J. Harmon

The addition of a garage or a carport to a one-story house can often afford a good opportunity to include a roof garden. The roof is approached not from the garage, of course, but by a penthouse built on the roof of the house. Since the garage is usually added near the utility area of the house next to the kitchen or family room, a small space in one of these rooms can be used for a stair to the penthouse.

A circular metal stair can be used to reach the penthouse from the kitchen if there is no space available for a regular staircase. The well for a prefabricated circular stair can be

Built during the French colonization in 1765, Acadian House, St. Martinsville, Louisiana, was designed in the "raised cottage" style, with a brick ground floor raising the main floor high in the air to protect it from water and dampness. Its raised porch could provide security in today's homes.

as small as 44 inches square. If possible, however, use a standard stair because children and the elderly sometimes have trouble navigating the narrow circular stairs.

The penthouse can even be carried across an open space such as a walkway if the garage is not attached to the house. Carports are very insecure places to store automobiles and are not recommended for most areas. They are really only covered driveways in most cases, over which a roof garden structure would be topheavy. There are instances, however, in which they can be useful as a protective entryway and provide for a secure roof garden too, when placed over the drive at the entrance in the form of the old porte-cochère.

SECOND-FLOOR PORCHES

When President Truman decided he wanted to add a second-floor porch to the south facade of the White House, he had the right thing in mind. When most people think of second-floor porches, they think of the wide verandas around all four sides of southern mansions and the airy iron grillework of the New Orleans French quarter, but their use is not limited to specific architectural designs.

Second-floor porches can be almost as secure as roof gardens although they do not have the advantage of giving you a view of all four sides of your property. Obviously, the second and biggest disadvantage of a second-floor porch is that it can be used by a prowler to get at bedroom doors and windows. Footsteps on a porch are not as likely as those on a roof garden to notify occupants who may be sleeping that someone is there.

To be secure, a second- or third-floor porch must be—or appear to the casual observer to be—inaccessible. Height, while a deterrent, is not enough. This is especially true of the average second-floor porch, only

The mere mention of New Orleans suggests wrought iron porches, such as this one on Royal Street completed in 1860 by James Gallier, Jr. Secure, and high above the sidewalk, the porches provide shade from the sun and shelter from the rain.

An upstairs porch with a solid railing creates an impression of height and is harder to scale than one with an open railing. A glass or plastic roof would make the porch usable in wet weather, protecting sliding glass doors to bedrooms, and still allowing ample light into the rooms.

eight or nine feet above the ground. For instance, just see if you cannot touch the ceiling in a standard eight-foot-high living room. The average man of five feet ten inches can extend his arms over his head to seven feet five inches. Most women can easily change a ceiling light bulb using a dining room chair to stand on. So you can see it does not take much of a jump to reach nine feet. Parked cars, windowsills, trellises, heavy vines, nearby trees—anything anyone can climb on to reach the porch will, of course, only make it easier.

When you build or remodel a second-floor porch, do not expose structural members beneath it close to the ground that will per-

This second-floor porch is made more secure by excavating the ground to a lower level. Living-room and basement windows are secured by a metal-wire fence, which also prevents animals and children from tumbling into the expanded light well.

mit anyone to get a handhold or foothold to climb up. Keep supporting columns smooth and without pedestals on which someone could get a foothold to boost himself or an accomplice up.

If you have solid railings for privacy, keep the exterior smooth and without any horizontal breaks that someone could hold on to. When an open railing is used, eliminate all horizontal elements and ornamentation except the handrail, and keep vertical members thin, straight, and high so they cannot be climbed.

A grille, of either wood or metal, can be placed around the open sides of the porch. The grille should be taken to the roof of the

A metal grille secures the open side of this second-floor porch. A matching metal gate in the ground floor opens so a car can be driven into the safety of the enclosure.

porch. If the porch is an open deck and not roofed, a similar grille can be used to cover it. In either case, an inconspicuous locked opening should be placed in the grille in case of an emergency. Or several openings could be left in the grille not large enough to get through, but large enough for someone to signal for help.

A rolling grille that can be pushed up out of the way and out of sight, but pulled down and locked, could also be used to secure the porch while still allowing for ventilation.

This, as all operable security measures, can be wired to an alarm.

Simple heavy wooden shutters can be used between the porch roof supports. These can be louvered or grilled for ventilation, hinged to swing open either from the sides or out from the top to provide additional and adjustable protection from the sun and rain.

If the porch is an unroofed deck, shutters can be used on the exposed walls supported by ceiling-high columns that can also sup-

The wooden grille of this porch eliminates the need for railings. The porch also provides cover for automobiles to the front door.

port an open wire grille over the top.

When the area under the porch off the second floor is to be enclosed and used as living space, the floor of the porch will have to be solid and waterproofed. A wood or concrete structure will require a membrane layer of waterproofing on top of the structure and under the finished floor similar to that used for roof gardens.

The floors of most wooden porches are least expensively made of planks separated by an air space about the width of a nail to allow water to drain and prevent the wood from rotting. This does not affect the security so much as the privacy of the porch. The open flooring will also permit air to circulate through the floor of the porch when the walls are closed up. However, nothing very permanent in the way of structure can be placed or built under the porch because of water drainage. Trees and planting should be kept to a minimum and cut back under the porch to prevent anyone's hiding there and to keep ground fire from spreading to the porch.

A. J. Harmon

A second-floor verandah was used extensively in Louisiana and called a galerie. It was also used before 1683 in such houses as Van Cortlandt Manor, Croton, New York.

A combination roof garden, porch, and sundeck with striped canvas awning, designed to resemble a boat deck. Access from lower floors is under stair at left, lighted by a round plastic bubble similar to the openings above the built-in sofa in the covered area.

An old Victorian classic can be made more secure with underground electric and telephone lines—the basic alarm system.

Chapter Eight

Alarms

For centuries the traditional alarm used by man to protect his home and possessions was his dog, who not only would bark to alert the household, but was very often quite capable of coping with the problem physically until additional help arrived. More unconventional guards have been hungry lions roaming the grounds at night behind high walls, crocodiles swimming in moats, any number of birds that can create a racket when disturbed, and even today trained attack dogs wandering empty halls. These dogs are much too dangerous to be used without a professional handler, and the average homeowner would be foolish to consider their use. They will attack the innocent as well as the burglar, and some very shrewd crooks are taking in more money selling badly bred and poorly trained dogs than they ever did breaking into houses. These dogs can attack their owners, and expensive lawsuits—rightly so—can sometimes result if the animal gets loose in a neighborhood.

A dog is still one of the best protections and alarm systems a house can have, provided he lives inside the house. Yard dogs can bark and make a lot of noise but by law, in most civilized neighborhoods, must be tied or fenced in where they are susceptible to bribes in the form of a steak or to silencing with drugs or poison. A dog inside the house can raise a fuss without being in immediate danger, but do not get a dog just to keep burglars away if you do not like animals. If they cannot be made part of the family, they are likely to welcome the first kind word from a stranger and leave with him as he carries out the family jewels—and who is to blame them?

Dogs do require care, tiny yipping terriers who bark all the time just as much as the dignified German shepherd that can be a real protection. Some people cannot be bothered with a dog or, if they can be, will take the pet along with them when they travel, to guard not only the car but themselves as well, thereby leaving the house unguarded. Of course, if you must choose, your person is more important than your possessions.

Your house can be guarded both when you are there and when you are away by any number of alarms and alarm systems. Magazines and newspapers are full of advertisements offering cheap burglar alarms. No package system is satisfactory, and some systems are worse than none at all because they instill a sense of security in the homeowner. Each alarm system must be custom designed and installed for your home and your way of life. Buy only from established local dealers who use well-known brand names. Continuing service to the alarms is necessary, and you do not want to have your entire system out of order for months while some minor replacement part sits on a dock in Yokohama.

You can buy an alarm system or you can lease one. To buy one will cost from $600 to $4,500, depending on how sophisticated it is. You can lease an alarm system for anywhere from $300 to $1,000 for the installation, with monthly service charges from $20 to $80 a month. Deal only with the most highly recommended and reliable local firms because the installer will be inside your house, will know where the alarms are, know how the system works and the best way to get around it. If I were going to become an expert burglar, I would get an installation job with the best security company in town.

By all means consult with the police department. They cannot recommend companies, but they can advise you on which systems are most satisfactory and which involve the fewest false alarms. Keep in mind, though, that the police want to catch criminals and may recommend silent alarms—those that notify only the police department

that a burglary is taking place, giving them time to get to the house to make an arrest. Most homeowners would rather not be in the middle of a shoot-out and prefer the kind of alarm that notifies the police and at the same time turns on all the house and garden lights, setting off sirens, bells, and what have you to frighten the burglars as far away as humanly possible.

Basically there are two kinds of alarm systems, wired and unwired. The unwired system uses sensors to send information to a central control by radio. These radio signals can be interfered with and the system difficult to control because you have no idea if the transmitters or batteries are working. In a wired system everything is tied together with wires.

These two systems break down into more categories, some very sophisticated and hardly for use in a residence, such as the capacitance detector, which sets up a low-power magnetic field around objects to be protected, such as the crown jewels. If anyone enters the area, all sorts of alarms go off.

There are systems based on electromagnetic microwaves and ultrasonic sound waves which detect movement in a room, but these are subject to many false alarms and can be activated by movement or noise in the next room, the starting up of an air conditioner or furnace. Most people cannot hear the sound waves, pitched too high for their ears; but pets, especially dogs, can and may be highly irritated by them, as can some humans without realizing it.

A system using photoelectric cells passing a beam of light between or an invisible infrared system with only one receiver can be used. However, these light-activated systems are subject to many false alarms, due to children and pets, and even to adults who are unaware or forgetful of their presence. A burglar, having done his research well, can climb either under or over the light beam.

Pressure detectors, thin pads used under

rugs and carpeted stairs, are good devices for revealing intruders, but if used only inside, they will be activated only after a prowler is already in the house—and what you want to do is keep him out. Pressure detectors are also subject to false alarms if, for instance, your cat stomps across one.

A pressure detector in the driveway—similar to those used in gasoline stations but concealed beneath the surface and connected by underground wiring to the house—and others in front of the entrance, back, and terrace doors can be used to alert you to guests or prowlers. These must be designed carefully to register only an automobile or truck coming up the drive and an adult at the door, or your house will be beeping like the control panel of a spaceship as the children run in and out of the house or charge down the driveway on their bicycles.

Metallic tape that carries a low-voltage electric current can be used to signal that an intruder has broken the glass in windows or doors. The tape must run continuously around the glass and has some value in windows that are small or that have removable mullions dividing the window into small sections—the mullions conceal the tape. It can also be used on tempered glass that crumbles into tiny pieces as now required on all sliding glass doors. Used on the perimeter of large plate-glass windows or doors it can be distracting, and any thief who is not high on drugs can easily use a glass cutter and a plumber's helper to remove a large central portion of the window without setting off the alarm.

To arm an alarm—that is, to turn on the system when you leave the house or retire at night—the master control must be turned on with a key, push button, or time-delay device. All have advantages and disadvantages, and which you choose will depend on what kind of a person you are and your habits.

The key control is somewhat inconve-nient, and you can lose the key or it can fall into the wrong hands. A push-button panel control with a digital combination is the more convenient, but you—and all family members—must remember the combination. The more people who know the combination, the less secure the system. The time-delay control is the most convenient.

Delayed-time devices which allow you 30 seconds to get in and out of the door allow the arming mechanism to be placed on the interior of the house where it cannot be tampered with, but many people underestimate their entrance and exit timing, which causes many false alarms—especially when they are just at the door and the telephone rings or they remember that they have forgotten the shopping list.

The master control panel should be placed out of sight, but where it can be reached quickly and easily. These operate on low voltage and have adapters so that they are in full operation with batteries in case of a power failure.

All security systems should include fire detection devices using either smoke or heat detectors. Most people prefer the smoke detector because a fire can have spread considerably before the temperature reaches the 120 to 130 degrees required in order to activate the heat detector.

You should also include panic buttons at the front door and the back door in case you answer the door and someone tries to force his way in. A third panic button should be placed on the night table in the master bedroom in the event you hear prowlers in the house, see them in the garden, or awake in the night and smell smoke or are ill.

Some security companies maintain 24-hour surveillance on houses and apartments, using microphones placed around the house and connected to a central office. The office monitors all sounds and conversations and alerts their private security guards and police if anything suspicious is heard. The transmitters can be switched off for privacy on request, provided the person doing the requesting identifies himself. Otherwise the police are instantly alerted. This sort of system, as most of them, is only as good as the company that maintains the security. The loss of privacy may seem a high price to pay for the privilege of being safe in your own home, but more and more people are willing to make the exchange. However, a monitoring system seems more applicable to a bank or store after hours when any noise is more likely to be suspicious in the supposedly deserted area.

Alarm and monitoring systems are being worked on that will operate through cable television wires, bringing television into your home and also allowing security precautions to be sent back through the cable to a central desk where an emergency situation can be recognized.

All of these systems or a combination of them can be connected to a central control panel that will set off gongs, sirens, or screamers, turn on interior and exterior floodlights, and at the same time notify the police or private agency to send help. You may not be permitted to be connected directly to the police station, but you can use a private agency or have the automatic control panel dial the police telephone number and deliver a prerecorded message giving your name and address and requesting immediate help. These can also automatically notify the fire department through heat and smoke detection devices that there is a fire in the house.

Some radio-controlled systems violate FCC regulations, so before you buy any system, make sure that there are no obstacles in effect or planned that would make the system illegal or inoperable.

The biggest problem with any alarm system is false alarms through carelessness, and you as the homeowner are the only one who can prevent them. They are so prevalent that most police departments—rightly—charge $25 to $50 for every false alarm they answer. Even if the system is not connected to the police or to a private security company and you only have a siren on your house, false alarms going off at all hours of the day and night can infuriate neighbors. At best such false alarms can get you cited for disturbing the peace, and at worst can encourage the neighbors to ignore you when you really do need help.

If only noise from a siren or gong is used to alert you and your family that prowlers are about and you are not connected to the police or a private security company, have the alarm placed on the front of the house facing the street, where it cannot be reached without a ladder, and encased in a locked steel box. This will give notice to anyone casing the house that an alarm system is installed and that it will be difficult to get to the alarm and disarm it by removing the clapper without tools, a ladder, and a chance of being seen from the street.

You should also have a small printed sign furnished by the installation company on every door and window saying something like THESE PREMISES ARE PROTECTED FROM BURGLARY BY ELECTRONIC SURVEILLANCE. The company should not be named because the housebreaker can call them pretending to be someone else and get needed information about the equipment and the system.

THE INTERCOM

An intercom system can be a help in protecting the security of your house by enabling you to identify the person at the front or back door. However, if you must choose between an intercom and a good new lock, take the lock. Too often the intercom is of nothing more than nuisance value as far as break-ins are concerned. A prowler can try to raise you through the intercom, and if no one answers, he can be almost sure your house is empty whether there are lights on or not.

It is also annoying to be at the beck and call of any passerby who wants to know if this is the Jones house, and of all traveling salesmen, canvassers, and passing children wanting to cut the grass, rake the leaves, wash the car, or shovel the snow. This is not to mention the teenagers who can invade quiet neighborhoods at night and use the intercom to simulate ghosts to frighten the baby-sitter at 11 P.M. or wake the entire family at 3 A.M.

THE TELEPHONE

Ma Bell is, of course, one of the biggest security systems in existence, although not that inexpensive anymore (consider that it may be cheaper to pay $100 or more a year when the house is closed down and the telephone is not in use than to have it turned off and reinstalled). Nevertheless, a house without a telephone is not secure because you cannot call out to get help, not only when you fear a burglar, but when you smell smoke or are ill and alone.

The telephone can also be used to give information to a housebreaker. If your name is on the mailbox and your number is listed, he can dial the number and know no one is home, regardless of how many lights were left burning if no one answers. Never give any information about yourself, your family, or your neighbors to anyone calling on the telephone.

If you can afford only one telephone, have it installed in the master bedroom so it rests on a night table next to the bed. Preferably you should have a separate line—not an extension—with an unlisted number there. This will prevent a burglar from taking another extension telephone off the hook so you cannot dial the police if you hear strange noises in another part of the house.

Keep a flashlight beside your bed and have police emergency and fire department numbers taped to the wall or telephone on a piece of paper protected by clear plastic. If there is a fire, the electricity can already be out. If a burglar is inside the house, you will not want to attract attention by turning on a light. Whoever it is, you do not want to meet him. He has to be crazy to be a crook in the first place.

Many times the telephone company is sloppy in running the telephone line to your house from the pole on the street. Why the utility and telephone companies are so primitive that they stick wires up on poles where wind, ice, falling trees, and crashing automobiles can knock them down is their secret. Get underground service for both if possible. If it is not, check to see if the wires are so close to the ground that they can be easily cut. Sometimes the first thing a criminal will do when attacking a house—and that is what it is, an attack—is to cut the light and telephone lines, cutting off any wired alarms and any way for you to reach outside help. If the telephone line is close to the ground, have the company raise it.

Builders always have the telephone installed as an afterthought, as if they expected you to communicate by carrier pigeon. The telephone installers are not carpenters and even if the line is raised high enough above the ground from the pole to the house, they will jiggle the telephone line down the side of the house, fastening it only with staples until they find a convenient entry location about hand-high so they do not have to bend, stoop, or stand on a ladder to get the line through the wall to the telephone. Make sure that the line enters the house at an inaccessible spot and that any line on the outside of the house is securely encased.

Check your telephone line. If you can get at it, so can anyone else. Have underground service if you can afford it. If not, have the line moved and enclosed so it cannot be cut.

An Early American Dutch door in the Van Deusen house in Hurley, New York, dating from 1723. The upper half opened independently to allow fresh air to enter without letting barnyard animals into the house.

Chapter Nine

Doors

The Egyptians had wooden pin tumbler locks on their doors two thousand years before Christ, and other locks and locking devices date back well before that time. In the Greek and Roman ruins of Paestum and Pompeii it is still possible to see the small rooms off the entrances to houses where a slave was kept, one foot chained to a metal ring in the floor with just enough tether to allow him to unbar the door any hour of the day or night after determining if he who knocked was welcome. This also saved the master of the house the trouble of having to carry a key around with him. Doors were barred at all times and only a small shuttered opening faced the street, permitting the slave to see who it was at the door and in the street beyond.

The slaves were eventually given their freedom, and better devices were developed to open the massive and otherwise impenetrable doors from the exterior. Even in the smallest cottages, security was dependent on a heavy door, locked and barred on the inside after nightfall, when few people ventured out.

Sicilian peasants have an ingenious way of protecting their doors and cottages from strangers. They plant heavily thorned cactus for quite a distance around the house. There is only one, almost invisible path, known only to the members of the family, winding through the barbed cactus. Try getting away with the family silver and television sets through that.

When the first settlers came to North America, they built their doors of heavy timber, their homes like small individual fortresses. This building of personal fortification continued until, as an emerging new nation, they were strong and secure enough to allow themselves the freedom to develop a more open style of building and architecture.

Early settlers in America built log cabins as individual fortresses. As the house evolved in this country it changed from fortification to precious crystal box with uninterrupted walls of glass. Now, with crises in security and energy, we have come full circle and are being forced to return to the protection of solid walls.

A portcullis in the entrance gate of a French château. The wood and metal door was lowered from the second floor by the gatekeeper to keep out strangers.

And during the last three decades we have seen house design change from a series of doors, walls, and windows into structures of nothing but sliding glass doors. However, because of the social and economic changes taking place, this era is coming quickly to an end, not only due to the lack of security and privacy involved but because these glass structures are more expensive to build, heat, air-condition, and ventilate.

Soon we will no longer be able to afford to build the splendid crystal boxes set in the center of green lawns. We will not be able to afford the water for the lawns and land occupied by decorative planting, the energy to keep the interiors a constant temperature winter and summer, or be able to waste the gasoline and highway construction to transport ourselves to these remote bedroom villages. When we cannot, our doors will once again assume the importance they had in the Middle Ages.

A traditional door in Williamsburg, Virginia, in the George Reid House, built between 1789 and 1792.

THE FRONT DOOR

In the days before gunpowder was invented, towns and castles alike had entrances protected by a drawbridge over a moat and a portcullis, which was a massive wood-and-metal overhead door that was let down in the gateway to prevent the road from being used. This entrance was one of the most important security elements in the architectural design, and the main thrust of any enemy was always concentrated here.

The Romans thought so much of the security of their homes that, although they prayed to many gods, the two most important were Vesta and Janus—Vesta, the goddess who protected the hearth and the household, and Janus, who guarded the door. Not at all strange when you consider that even today more than half of all burglaries take place during the day and al-

A medieval English door from Norwich dating from about 1300. The heavy planks are made more secure and more attractive by handsome ironwork which binds the planks together.

most half of those are through the front door.

Every house should have a back door as well as a front door as a safety measure in case of emergency. However, the front door is the most important door in the house. From the standpoint of security, it is usually the most obvious door, the easiest one to get to, and is ordinarily connected to the driveway—at least, it should be. It is the door first tried—"cased," if you want, by a prospective burglar posing as a salesman,

priest, policeman, or almost anything else.

The front door is also crucial in establishing the design and character of your house, not only in the way it looks but in the way it feels and sounds. The design of the door, the color and the hardware, can change the atmosphere of the entrance from sophisticated to provincial. Among the Pennsylvania Dutch, a blue door meant that a daughter of marriageable age lived in the house. The Japanese would not even consider a white door because white symbolizes death; plain,

A medieval Spanish door dating from about 1400 in Burgos, reinforced and tied together with iron through the planks. A small door within the larger opening permits entry without exposing the entire area.

pure white is almost never worn in Japan except by converted Christians and, even then, rarely.

A highly lacquered black door or a polished dark stain is appropriate for an elegant city house but would look out of place on a country cottage, unless, of course, it happened to be a château. A sophisticated provincial door can be plain white, a mellowed stain, or a soft color complementing the exterior.

The design of the door should reflect the period and style of the house and the interior. Colonial doors can be English, French, Dutch, or Spanish, all of a number of different periods. Doors can also be given any style and character you want—changing the atmosphere from English to French, for instance—simply by the selection of the hardware.

Most hardware manufacturers make at least one expensive but good line of hardware along with the cheap lines they sell to builders. The trouble is that very few manu-

This home, built by John Palmer in 1754 on Duke of Gloucester Street in Williamsburg, has double louver doors on the entrance for protection during the summer, when the entrance door was left open for air to circulate.

facturers make good-looking hardware, although it may be good enough to keep out the opportunistic amateur. Usually the handsomest is the most expensive, such as American colonial of the simplest design in black. It must be wrought iron or the black will wear off with use. (The design is really English colonial, but at one time there were more of them here than anywhere else, so it became American colonial.)

Good hardware is expensive and cheap hardware is a waste of money both for security purposes and for appearance. It will fall apart and have to be replaced in a few years. The feel of a good doorknob and the solid sound that a heavy, well-balanced, and perfectly fitted door makes are very important not only for you and your guests, but for the impression they make on a burglar. He is going to go through the door only once, and if it is too much trouble, he can decide not to make the effort. You are going to use your door every day, many times a day, perhaps for years, and you should make it a pleasant experience every time.

Incidentally, after giving a lot of thought

A contemporary adaptation of á louvered and screened door that would permit the front door to be opened during the day for ventilation. Light is admitted to the entrance hall through the fixed glass in the slit transom.

and spending a sizable amount of money on a front door that helps establish the character of the house, do not throw all the effort and money down the drain by covering it with an aluminum storm or screen door. I have never seen an attractive one, and they cheapen any facade they are on. Get a good, solid exterior door, have it weatherstripped, and allow it to be part of the design of the house.

If you feel you must have a storm door, you can use a heavy louvered and screened door that will cover the front door. Re-

member, however, that this door will have to swing out and any door that swings out is easier to jimmy. Unless invisible hinges and sturdy hardware are used, it is simple for a burglar to pull the hinge pins out to get to the front door.

A louvered screen door will allow you to ventilate with some security in the summer, since a thief cannot see through and the louvers are difficult to break quietly; he will be deterred, but only if the door is kept locked. Of course, no door is going to keep out a determined and experienced burglar;

An old well-fitting door with unsafe glass can be made safe with heavy planks. The hinges here are for decoration, but new hardware will be needed because of the added weight and thickness of the remodeled door.

but a good door, tightly fitted and with good hardware, will discourage transients and young sneak thieves.

In contrast, the aluminum combination storm and screen doors have latches that can be opened in about three minutes from the outside. Even if they have additional locks on them, the soft metal will bend like a tin can under pressure from a screwdriver. They also create a sense of false security in summer months if kept locked during the day or night when the front door is left open for ventilation.

Any front door that has glass in it, regardless of the quality of the locks, should either be thrown away and replaced with a solid door or, if the panes are small with heavy muntins dividing them, have the glass replaced with wire glass or a break-resistant glass. You should see who is at the door before opening it, but a small wide-angle lens placed in the door serves this purpose better than any window can.

Standard paneled doors offer very little

Heavy permanent shutters fixed over the sidelights will make this entrance more secure while still allowing a small amount of light into the entrance hall.

protection because the panels can be quickly cut away or, in the case of cheap doors, simply pushed in. You can either get a new solid door or sheathe the old door in plywood screwed and glued to the existing door (see Chapter 4). You will then need heavier hinges and a new, deeper lock, but if the existing door is inexpensive, the hardware will be, too, and will need changing.

Rickety and loose-fitting doors, often used by builders to speed construction, need to be replaced. They can be forced or jimmied open with very little pressure, and chances are the hardware is of very poor quality.

Double doors are very insecure. You can improve the security and retain the appearance by making one of the doors stationary (see Chapter 4).

Dutch doors, however romantic, cannot be locked securely and can usually be jiggled open because of the shrinking of the wood and the settling of the house.

Doors and entrances with sidelights inside or outside the door are a double hazard since

Glass sidelights such as these present a serious security problem that should be corrected with break-resistant glass, fixed shutters, or panels.

they reveal the interior of the house and can be broken quickly, easily, and noiselessly. If, because of the appearance of your entrance, you feel you must have them, replace the glass with wire glass or with small panes of tough break-resistant glass. Curtain or shutter the sidelights on the interior to prevent strangers from seeing through into the entrance hall.

When light is required or desired on the interior, small lights can be used in a transom over, not in or beside, the door with relative safety.

Some additional safety and privacy can be had with sidelights without too much loss of the character of the entrance if they are covered by heavy exterior shutters. However, these must be screwed deeply into structural members of the house with unremovable screws or they can be quickly removed, the glass broken, and the house entered.

Front doors that are approached through a screened or glazed porch are particularly vulnerable to a burglar because he can take all the time he needs to break through the most secure lock in the cover of the porch. He is protected from view both from the house and from the street. Porches and Florida rooms enclosed with jalousie windows and doors are particularly defenseless and there is no way of burglarproofing them except with bars.

THE ENTRANCE

The location of the front door is of particular importance for security. It need not be on the front of the house, but it should be visible from the street, unenclosed by walls, and not hidden by shrubbery. You should not give a thief the opportunity to work away on the door out of sight of the street and passing neighbors. The door should be quickly and easily reached from the driveway and from where the car is parked.

A dangerous and inhospitable entrance hidden from the street and drive. Poor lighting, glazed door and sidelights, and windows that allow surveillance present obvious disadvantages.

All of the foundation planting with which we smother our houses, especially Early American and colonial designs, was unheard of when America was a colony. Planting was kept away from the house as too easy a place for Indians or outlaws to hide and pounce when you entered or left the house. Even later, when Georgian and Federal architecture were in vogue, foundation planting was kept to a minimum so the delicate and elegant detail of the design was not covered up.

Regardless of how romantic the vine-covered cottage sounds or looks, get rid of any planting around the door and the house itself that could conceal someone waiting in the shadows. An attacker does not need much intelligence or imagination to hide in the bushes until you come home and let you have it on the head while you pause to unlock the door. He can roll you into the house and make off with your valuables in your own car.

Your headlights should shine on the door when you return at night both to frighten an intruder away and so that you can be forewarned if the door is ajar or shows signs of having been tampered with. This gives you a chance to drive off for help instead of entering the house and coming face to face

Simple and effective entrances can be protected from weather by a covering such as this one on the Potts House, built about 1760 in Valley Forge.

with a burglar. Most professional burglars want to avoid confrontation and will leave quickly, but armed robbers and drug addicts may react dangerously in incomprehensible ways.

Most nighttime break-ins occur between 7 P.M. and midnight, so a well-lighted front door is imperative, not only for when you arrive home after dark, but so anyone at the door can be easily identified before you open it.

Two lights, one on each side of the door, are necessary. A single light on one side or over the door will throw a person's face in shadow or hide it completely with the aid of

a hat. The lights should be at eye level far enough from the door so that they cannot be stumbled into and should contain no sharp edges or corners that could injure the innocent. Often side lights are placed high on the wall because they are made of sharp, cheap metal. This not only makes them dangerous if placed low, but also makes replacing bulbs difficult. Make sure before you buy light fixtures that you can change the bulbs easily with one hand without having to stand on a ladder, that the material will not rust or corrode, and that there are not little screws to be taken out that can fall to the ground and be lost in the dirt or snow.

Enclosed lighting fixtures are designed to burn a maximum-wattage bulb. If there is no additional lighting near the door, get fixtures that will handle 100-watt bulbs. Using bulbs of higher wattage than the fixtures were designed for creates a fire hazard, and the bulbs will burn out rapidly.

Some cover over the entrance is desirable to keep rain away from the door. A sheltered entrance lets you stand under cover to unlock the door and keeps your guests from having to wait at the door in the rain. The steps should be clearly lighted and have a handrail for support.

THE BACK DOOR

A back door should never be designed to exit into the garage. There can be a door from the house to the garage, but there should also be another door to the exterior.

Everything that has been said about the front door applies equally to the back door, but special attention should be given to its security because so many women prefer to have about half of the back door glazed to get additional light in the kitchen and to keep an eye on youngsters playing in the back yard.

Wire or break-resistant glass should replace any glazed section of the back door and the lock should be just as tamperproof and secure as the one on the front door. The principles of strong lighting and no heavy foundation planting must be observed even more stringently around the back door because of its location.

The back door has the added problem of almost never facing the street, thus enticing to housebreakers. It would be ideal if the front door faced the street and the back door was on the driveway visible from the street, but this is seldom the case.

A back door sheltered by a pent roof and made more secure by trimmed planting and good lighting. The window can be protected by a heavy shutter, and break-resistant glass installed in the door.

An open heavy wooden timber passage from the back door to the drive makes this back entrance safer and does not cut off light and air from windows. Heavy wire and rose bushes protect the top and discourage access to the second-floor windows.

You can, however, sometimes create a new back door on the drive or in a more secure location by adding a hallway, which can serve as a pantry, reaching from the existing kitchen door to an entry on the driveway. This will add storage space and a more secure back entrance. If the addition of a pantry would block out light and ventilation from windows in other rooms of the house, the passage can be built of open concrete block or as a heavy timber trellis. If

light is the only problem, the passage can be built of glass blocks.

A connecting door between the house and an attached garage is particularly tempting to anyone wanting to break in; he can take his time, using the garage to protect him from the street and neighbors. The usual overhead garage door latch is no match for a professional burglar, and garage windows are usually not fitted with anything more than the standard twist latch provided by the

The toughest and most secure passage from the back door to the drive is one built of glass block, which provides light and insulation. Additional light and air can be had through ventilating skylights in the roof.

manufacturer. Both the door and windows should be fitted with additional keyed locks.

You should not store tools and ladders in the garage as so many people do. Once inside the garage, a prowler can use your own tools to break through the connecting door or can carry a ladder out to the back of the house and get at an upstairs window.

The connecting door between the garage and the house must, by law, be a metal-clad fire door, but do not be deluded because it is metal on one side; this is to keep a fire, not people, from spreading too rapidly into the house. Since the burglar will have the time he needs, the shelter of the garage, and any number of tools at hand, buy the best door you can and equip it with the most suitable locks you can afford. If you have to settle for fewer alarms, this is the door at which one should be placed, to alert the neighbors and the police. The ringing alone can be enough to scare off intruders.

Overhead garage doors are usually divided into four panels and can be made less conspicuous with siding and paint matching that of the house and garage.

THE GARAGE DOOR

Our garage doors in many ways resemble the portcullises used for centuries to close off the entrances to cities and castles. Yet, because of flimsy construction and poor locks, they do not offer us the security they should.

There should be no windows in the garage door. It is too easy for a prowler to look in to see if your car is there or if the garage is empty, indicating that the family is away. If your garage door does have glazing in it, you can either put paint on the glass panels or place extra paneling over the entire door, making it stronger at the same time. The garage will have windows in it, but these can be curtained or shuttered so no one can see the interior.

Standard garage hardware is not adequate and you should have an additional dead lock installed. Key locks should be installed on all garage windows, but they should never be nailed closed. There will be times when

Avoid garage doors with glass that a snooper can see through. Windows can be covered with molding and trim.

they are required for ventilation—when an automobile is being worked on or the garage is being used to paint something and it is either too cold or too windy to keep the overhead door open.

On attached garages, an automatic garage door is a good security measure as well as a great convenience. Operated from inside the car, you can avoid any prowlers lurking in the shadows as well as eliminate the sometimes forgotten chore of closing the garage door. Garage doors should always be

closed, not only because an open garage without an automobile in it notifies everyone that you are out, but because the gaping opening is ugly.

When you buy an automatic garage door, make sure the installation includes automatic lighting so the lights in the garage come on when the door opens, remain on long enough for you to get into the house, and then turn themselves off. There should be a security switch you can throw so the door can be opened only from the inside of

Sliding glass doors are the most vulnerable part of any security system. This one is protected with old-fashioned plank doors with concealed hinges. Dead bolts on the top and bottom of each door slide into head and base. Additional brackets can hold a two-by-four or a metal bar so the doors cannot be forced open.

the garage. The door should have an automatic reversal system that will send the door back up if it encounters any obstacle such as your mother-in-law or the trunk of your car, but will disengage and let the door continue to close if it hits snow or ice that might have accumulated under the door. There should also be a simple system of operating the door manually in case of power failure.

There are two ways to activate automatic overhead doors. One is with a button-operated radio you carry with you in the car, similar to the remote controls available for television sets. These doors, however, can sometimes be accidentally activated by an airplane or by a passing automobile.

Overcoming this problem, but slightly less convenient because it requires that you come to a complete stop and reach out the window, is the key-operated opener. The opener is placed on a stanchion within arm's reach of the driver's side of the car and a key is inserted in it to open the door.

The area in front of the garage door should be lighted by fixtures with on-off switches in both the house and the garage and by floodlights that come on automatically when the overhead door is opened.

Barn-door hardware holds this protective door, made of two-by-fours, that slides across the opening and is held in place with a dead bolt through an angle iron at the bottom. The design has the advantage of securing the door while allowing light and air to enter.

SLIDING GLASS DOORS

The weakest link in any security system is usually the aluminum sliding glass doors leading from the house to the terrace. The lock amounts to absolutely nothing and the door can be either pushed or pulled until the lock gives or it can be opened with a small screwdriver. The large glass area reveals whether the contents of the room are expensive or not worth stealing and the coming-and-going habits of the family living there.

No self-respecting burglar is going to fool around the front door in full view of the street and the neighbors when all he has to do is walk around the corner of the house to the terrace door and open it with a screwdriver or a crowbar. The soft aluminum will give almost like putty. Lazier vandals can simply put several strips of tape over the glass, wrap a sock over a rock, almost silently break the glass, and walk in.

The so-called broomstick-in-the-track device, a piece of wood wedged across the stationary door, is no protection at all except from witless vandals. Even the more expensive wood sliding doors have several inches of play in the frame of the door for leveling,

Tamper-proof metal security doors can roll down from the top, such as the solid one on the left, or across the opening, such as the one on the right. They can be operated either manually or electrically.

and although the door is wood, the sliding tracks are aluminum and can be flattened at the top and bottom of the door with a crowbar. This will allow the door to slide over the broomstick "stop bar" or under anything at the top of the door. The aluminum is not strong enough to resist bending.

There are various alarms that you can place on sliding glass doors to alert you if they are tampered with. These can be individual alarms on each door or alarms connected to a central system.

All building codes now specify that sliding glass doors must be glazed with tempered

glass. This will break, but it crumbles into tiny pieces and does not shatter into the dangerous jagged fragments that in the past have injured so many people. Once it is pierced, as with a glass cutter, the entire surface breaks. This means that metallic tape connected to an alarm works well on tempered glass. The tempered glass precludes the possibility of anyone's bypassing the metallic tape by holding the glass in place with a plumber's helper and cutting out a section with a glass cutter. Older glass doors, however, may not be made of tempered glass.

French door, such as this one at Parlange, Louisiana, built in 1759 can be made safer with dead bolts at the head and the sill.

Some sliding glass doors have grilles to simulate small panes in the glass. If the grilles are removable for cleaning, metallic tape can be hidden under them so that no section of glass large enough to enter can be broken without breaking the tape. Such grilles can be used if the door is glazed with something other than tempered glass. However, in most cases, you will be better off replacing the glass.

French doors, the much more attractive predecessors of sliding glass doors, are usually easier to make secure because of their stronger construction. The small panes of glass will have to be replaced with break-resistant glass or thick plastic glass. Small pieces of plastic glass are tougher to break; on the other hand, the plastic can burn and melt. Plastic scratches more easily, but it is acceptable for the small panes of French doors where the inevitable scratches will not be so noticeable.

Use a laminated steel padlock equipped with hasps at the top and bottom of French doors. Keyed dead-bolt locks can also be used on each door at the floor. These can be forced, but not without creating a lot of noise.

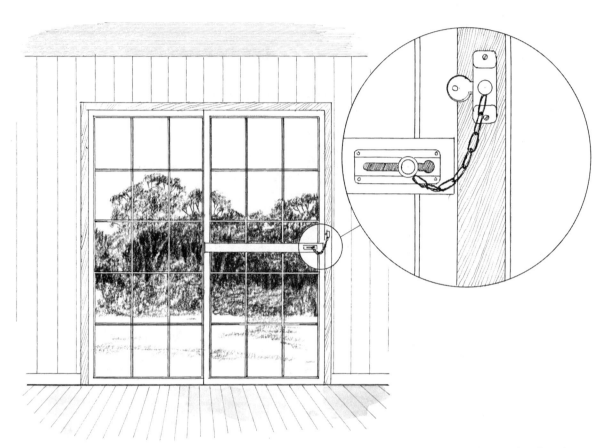

Sliding glass doors can be made to provide more protection by replacing the glass with wire glass or break-resistant glass. You can also install a bar across the center of the movable section provided with a dead lock and a keyed chain-door lock (shown enlarged).

Plastic glass is tough to break, but its use in the large sheets required in sliding glass doors is questionable because, given its size and the poor construction of the door, it can be bent out of the frame.

The situation with so-called unbreakable glass can be a problem. No glass is unbreakable. There is bulletproof glass, which is made by building up different layers of materials and is used in banks and to surround presidential swimming pools, but it is very thick, enormously expensive, and out of the question for the average homeowner.

Sliding glass doors can have the glass replaced with laminated tempered glass. There is laminated glass like that used in automobiles, but it can be broken. There is plastic glass that can be used in sliding doors that is some seventeen times as strong as regular glass, but it too can be broken. It scratches so easily that it takes only about a year to become so foggy you can hardly see through it. You can also burn a hole in it.

To secure the sliding door, install a crossbar on the operable door at the center of the door parallel to the floor, with a keyed

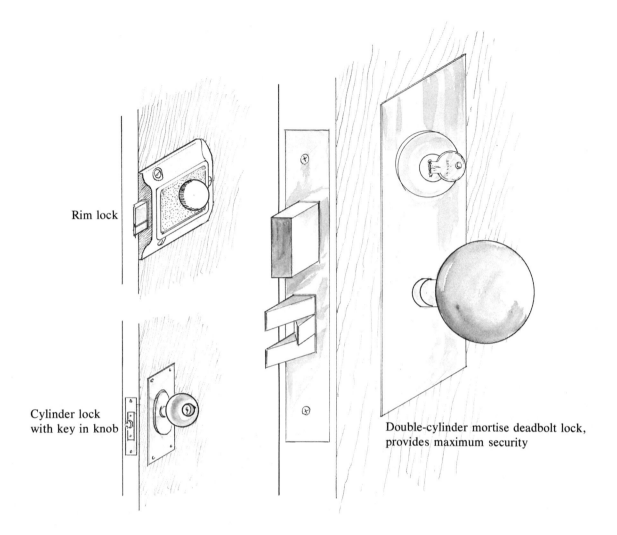

Rim lock

Cylinder lock
with key in knob

Double-cylinder mortise deadbolt lock,
provides maximum security

chain lock well anchored to the frame. A sliding glass door can also be secured with a sliding overhead metal grille, but to be really effective the grille and container should be built into the structure during construction.

LOCKS

There are basically three kinds of locks for your door: mortise, cylindrical, and rim locks. Of these, only mortise locks are suit-able for any kind of security at your doors, and you must be very selective in choosing them.

Only a mortised steel-clad, ten-lever-mechanism lock with a dead bolt that has a throw of at least one inch will give your doors the security they need. You will also need a keyed chain guard set with deep screws.

The exterior doors of your house should be at least 1¾ inches thick. The mortise lock is embedded in the door. Some of these locks must be unlocked from the inside with

An unattractive and dangerous entrance made worse by an ugly aluminum storm and screen door covering the "Poppa Bear, Momma Bear, Baby Bear" front door. Solid railings and high planting provide cover for prowlers. Second-floor windows can be reached from the porch roof.

a key, so care must be taken not to lock yourself inside in case of an emergency. Some also require that, as an extra security precaution, duplicates of the key can be made only at the factory and must be registered.

Mortise locks with automatic spring latches with stop works should not be used because they provide no security and can be easily opened from the outside. These latches are held in place with only a spring and can be pushed aside from the exterior. Never use any lock with a spring latch.

Cylindrical locks, sometimes called bore-in tubular locks or, commonly, key-in-the-knob locks, are the cheapest you can get and

After remodeling, the entrance is safe, and more attractive. With the porch removed second-floor windows are less accessible to a burglar. Sidelights around the door have been replaced with a new entrance that allows light into the hall through the transom. A heavy louver screen door covers the old glazed door, which has been reinforced with plywood. Shutters and window boxes give added protection.

offer no protection because of their poor quality and design. They can easily be forced; sometimes just turning the doorknob backwards will break them. Replace all of these immediately.

Rim locks are considered secondary locks and are only screwed to the surface of the door. They are easily forced and depend on the screws and the strength of the door frame for protection. Keyed chain locks are also of this type and should not be depended on for security from break-in. They are only a deterrent that permits you to communicate and receive mail through the small opening provided by the chain without having to unlock the door completely.

On the crowded narrow streets of old Spain, windows such as this medieval Andalusian window of the fourteenth century substituted for balconies. Raised high on their socle bases and enclosed with wrought iron, they also provided maximum security.

Chapter Ten

Windows

Without glass, there would be no windows; there would just be holes in walls for light and ventilation. Glass has been made by man for the last six thousand years. It was used in monastery and cathedral windows in the Middle Ages. But it was not until the late 1600s, when a process for casting it in larger sheets was developed in France, that it began to be used in private homes to any great extent. The Egyptians had small objects of glass in 2500 B.C., and perfume bottles have been found that date back to 1580-1350 B.C., but glass was not used for windows. In fact, windows played a very small part in the Egyptian house because sun and heat were best kept out with heavy solid walls.

In other periods of history people had a completely different concept than we have today of what the architectural design of a house was all about. After most of Rome burned down very early in the first century, with the exception of the roof structure and the half-timber construction of Europe and England, masonry was used almost exclusively not only for the construction of houses, but for the walls surrounding the towns. There were no such things as front and back yards exposed to the street, and certainly never any creeky little dank spaces between houses. The land in the walled town could not be wasted in the way we do today.

Houses were built right next to each other around courtyards, with the outer walls directly on the street and fire walls between them. The design of the house focused on the courtyard, a cool, quiet, secure retreat from the hot, dusty, crowded street. Any ground-floor windows that faced the street were small and placed high in the wall. They were used only to see who might be at the door or for ventilation in an unimportant

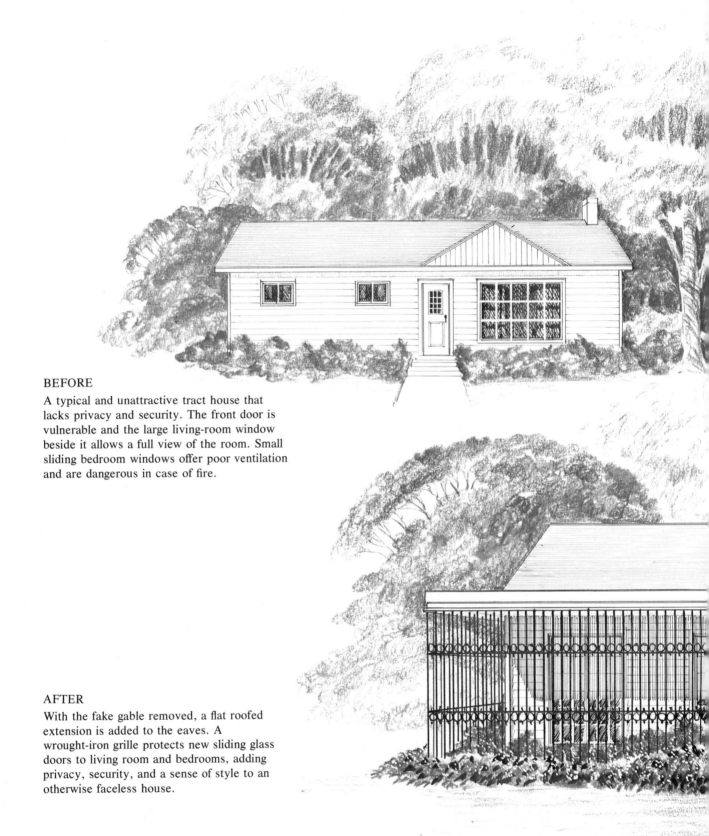

BEFORE

A typical and unattractive tract house that lacks privacy and security. The front door is vulnerable and the large living-room window beside it allows a full view of the room. Small sliding bedroom windows offer poor ventilation and are dangerous in case of fire.

AFTER

With the fake gable removed, a flat roofed extension is added to the eaves. A wrought-iron grille protects new sliding glass doors to living room and bedrooms, adding privacy, security, and a sense of style to an otherwise faceless house.

WINDOWS | 167

Inside the grilled overhang, even the tract house takes on exciting new character. The new living-room and bedroom sliding glass doors are secure and protected from the weather.

room, and were barred. Other windows on upper floors facing the street were securely shuttered at night, a custom that continues to this day in Europe, the East, and South America. There, even tall modern apartment buildings have metal shutters on all the windows. These are closed at night, not only for security, privacy, and quiet, but to keep out the night air, which many still believe to be evil, rendering a pox on the unlucky breather. And, with the foul air in the cities of today, they may be right.

The Romans did have some glass windows, but glass did not come into its own until the great Gothic cathedrals were built in the late twelfth century. The pieces of glass were small and held together with thin strips of lead used to mount them between heavy stone mullions. By the end of the fifteenth century glass began to appear in private houses, sometimes only in the upper half of the window. The lower half was covered with heavy wooden shutters.

All the windows in the Gothic and Renaissance architecture of the time were either fixed—that is, they did not open at all—or they were casement windows hinged on one side to open like a door. The window frame was filled with leaded glass, so called because of the lead strips holding the glass in place. Even after the end of the seventeenth century, when glass could be poured in large sheets, the panes were quite small by today's standards and the diamond-shape or rectangular sheets had to be spaced in the window frame with lead or wooden muntins which give the facades of our houses the indelible style, scale, and appeal that has come down to us in the distinctive American colonial designs that are still copied.

Of course, we can produce enormous sheets of glass today and build entire walls of buildings with it, but when these large sheets of glass are placed in traditional residential windows they give any house a dull open stare. It is not only the blankness of the unbroken glass sheets, but the lack of solid walls, lack of privacy, scale, space for furniture, and, of course, the massive problem of security that we are faced with.

Generally speaking, the thin muntins dividing the panes in standard wood windows offer no security because the glass is puttied in from the exterior and the muntins are easily snapped to enlarge the opening. The putty needs to be, and should be, replaced every several years because it dries and can be picked away with a penknife or stick. Heavier muntins could increase the security of the window, but they are not manufactured because in the past people placed the emphasis on light and the view.

Provided they have keyed locks on them as most windows should, windows with

This "sitting window" of Little Wenham Hall, Suffolk, in medieval England was built between 1270 and 1280 when use of leaded glass in windows of houses was becoming more commonplace.

The origins of the oriel window can be traced back to fortifications such as these turrets (bartizans) on Glamis Castle in Scotland, so guards could have a view of side walls without exposing themselves.

When fortifications became obsolete the bartizans evolved into oriel windows like this one over the entrance to Bramshill House, Hants, England.

metal muntins offer greater security since they are harder to break through even if the glass is removed.

However, the most important thing to remember in buying windows or making them secure is that the more difficult it is to get into the window from the outside, the more difficult it is going to be to get out. Do not create a trap for yourself or your family by making it hard to escape in a fire or other emergency. Keys can be lost, combinations forgotten, and even the simplest release mechanisms confused when one is alarmed and anxious, especially the young and the elderly, who are the most numerous victims of fires in private houses.

Never have only high windows in bedrooms. There must be a window that a child can crawl to, stand in front of, and through which he can be seen from the outside. The child may not be able to get out, but at least his location can be identified and help can be

An oriel window, here in the form of a standard bay window with a seat, is a delightful and secure addition to any room.

sent. Cheap, flimsy windows four or five feet off the floor are no more invulnerable to prowlers than any other kind and do create a serious hazard for anyone using the room.

Air-conditioning gives you the opportunity to keep the windows closed and therefore locked and more secure. Certainly the security air-conditioning offers makes it almost mandatory in cities and crowded suburbs. However, air-conditioning units that have been installed in double-hung windows with the bottom of the window in a raised position to accommodate the unit should be removed and installed through the wall under or beside the window. Windows propped open for an air-conditioning unit cannot be locked securely. Many times the unit can be removed easily either to enter the house or to steal the air conditioner. To have the unit moved to a through-the-wall location is not expensive when measured against the increase in security.

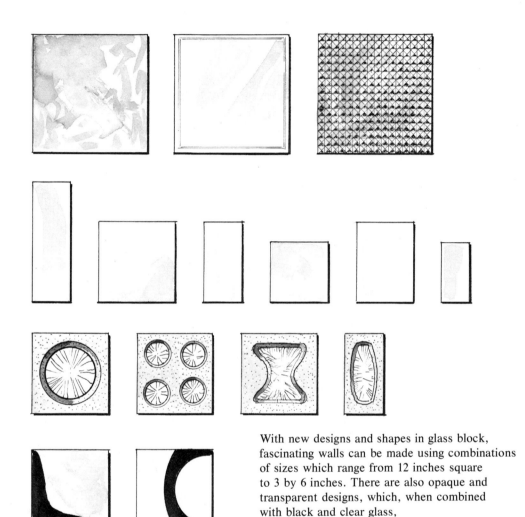

With new designs and shapes in glass block, fascinating walls can be made using combinations of sizes which range from 12 inches square to 3 by 6 inches. There are also opaque and transparent designs, which, when combined with black and clear glass, can be used to create three-dimensional walls.

FORMS

There are a number of different kinds of windows. The casement window is the oldest in existence, and it and the double-hung window are still the two most used windows today. Nonetheless, neither of these kinds of windows evolved or was designed for security, and there are other ways of getting light and ventilation into our houses without throwing them wide open to the street.

Glass Block Windows

Long neglected, there is no more secure way of getting light into a house than with glass blocks. They were quite the rage in the 30s, when every saloon and beauty parlor from Maine to Mexico threw up a "modernistic" front. However, some good uses were made of them, and we should not dismiss glass blocks as a building material. Handled carefully, they can produce quite handsome results.

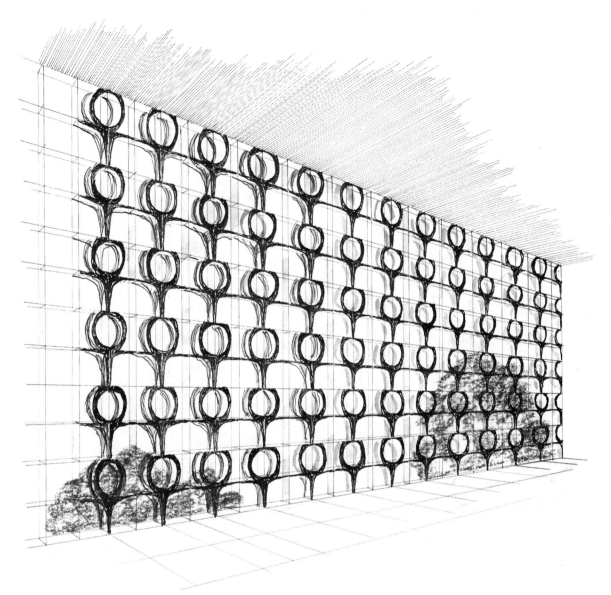

Taking the last two black and transparent glass blocks from the previous page, a three-dimensional grille can be created within the solid wall of glass.

No longer are they only plain, with a surface like ice cubes, or ribbed; they are now available in a variety of designs that combine style and color in squares and rectangles of many sizes. Different sizes can be combined to produce any number of attractive results.

Glass block is not load-bearing and cannot be expected to carry the weight of roofs or of upper floors. While not exactly a do-it-yourselfer's dream, glass block is not really much more difficult to lay than brick. Mortar and temperature-expansion strips and anchor strips must be used, but other than that, building a wall of glass block is similar to masonry construction using quarter-inch joints. The work is slow because only a few courses can be set at once to prevent mortar from being squeezed out of lower blocks by the weight of the blocks on top.

Glass block has the advantage of being about the most secure outside light you can

Clerestory windows at the intersection of two roof planes provide protection while still permitting light and air to enter into interior hallways and rooms.

provide for your home. As a window it does not need to be cleaned or curtained or draped, as a wall it does not need to be painted or maintained. It is fireproof, with an insulating value equal to or better than that of insulating glass.

Clerestory Windows
Usually placed between two intersecting roof planes, clerestory windows were used by the ancient Egyptians thousands of years before Christ for light and to allow the warm air next to the ceiling to escape, thus cooling the room. Not filled with glass until much later, they were covered with woven mats. In later ages they were sometimes covered with thin sheets of alabaster to allow light into the temples.

Clerestory windows have the advantage of being difficult to get to, usually only with a ladder and over another roof. If the windows are properly placed for security, using them for entry can be an obvious and noisy procedure. For additional security, the windows can be wired to an alarm if they are large enough to permit entry, securely

Fixed windows are the least expensive and can be used in combination with operable windows or doors for unusual or irregular spaces.

barred since they will not be used as an escape in case of fire, or combined with glass blocks to light and to ventilate interior hallways and rooms.

Fixed Windows

These are glazed openings in walls and the least expensive way to let light into a room. They have no moving parts and do not open or close so do not need to have locks. Generally used in combination with another type of window to provide ventilation, they are simply glass used as a wall. Rooms using fixed windows with no other means of ventilation will require use of year-round air-conditioning.

Fixed glass walls should have some means, such as a railing, of identifying themselves as walls, and not doors, so that people do not become confused and walk into them. For this reason too, they should always be made of tempered laminated glass, or plastic that will not shatter.

Used imaginatively, fixed windows have their place, but too often their extensive use

Awning windows made of wood, opened and closed with a self-locking crank, are secure, but probably one of the least attractive windows available.

makes heating and air-conditioning costs soar. And, there is something quite frustrating and irritating about being able to see out of a window but not being able to open it to let in fresh air.

Fixed glass should be installed from the interior into rabbeted jambs with stops nailed only on the interior. This is not only better water and weather protection, but prevents anyone from gaining entrance by removing the stops and lifting out the glass.

Depending on the location of fixed windows, cleaning can be relatively simple or almost impossible. It can be quite a chore when they are used on upper floors or in clerestories, or even on ground floors where they are behind a lot of close foundation planting. In these instances it is better to use opaque glass that will not show dirt or that needs only hosing down from the outside.

Awning Windows

These are windows in horizontal series hinged at the top and swinging out from the bottom. They are opened and closed with a crank that provides its own locking system, although for additional security a key lock

Metal awning windows are the most secure available. Fitted with vertical muntins, they present a better scale and appearance when closed.

can be fitted on one of the sections. Because the sections swing out, they must support their own weight and their construction is therefore much heavier than that of most other windows. Also, because they swing out horizontally, they must be cleaned more often, although they do provide good protection from the rain and fair ventilation. Screens are on the inside of the window; some people find this objectionable because dust and dirt collected on the screens will rub off on the curtains and draperies.

Awning windows are the most secure you can buy. Their construction, whether of metal or wood, must be heavier than that of other windows. They are difficult to break into; open or closed, they present an obstacle that is quite irksome to get through without spending a lot of time and making a lot of noise. The smaller the sash, the more troublesome the window is to navigate. One or two large sashes will not present the deterrent of a series of smaller ones.

The disadvantage of an awning window is its unattractiveness. The heavy horizontal sections hide the view; no matter where you happen to be standing or sitting, there always seems to be some division between

Casement windows in either metal or wood are relatively good protection. Operated with a self-locking gear, they swing out and provide 100 percent ventilation.

you and what you want to look at, so that your head must be in constant motion to get a clear view. Architecturally, they present a commercial appearance, although some metal designs are a bit lighter and the manufacturers have inserted vertical muntins in an attempt to achieve a better scale and a colonial-sash likeness.

Casement Windows
Casement windows are hinged on one side like a door, and the sash is operated with a gear and crank to swing them out. The crank provides its own locking device, but an additional lock can be provided. The gears on some of the newer models are made of aluminum and have a tendency to strip themselves and become inoperable within a week's time after installation. Get an extra handle crank for every three windows.

Some manufacturers claim that the casement can be cleaned from the interior, but it can be very difficult to get your arm through the opening between the sash and the frame. Removable grilles make the windows easier to clean and give better scale to the facade when used with colonial designs.

Double-hung windows, standard in most houses, can be made safer with good locks and break-resistant glass. The twist lock provided by the manufacturer is a security risk.

Casement windows open a hundred percent of the window for ventilation, although control can be difficult. Another advantage of casement windows is their appearance.

From a security standpoint, casement windows rank fairly well, much better than double-hung windows, but if a prowler can break the glass to get to the release and gear, they cannot compare with awning windows for keeping people out.

Double-hung Windows
Both the top and bottom sashes are operable in a double-hung window, allowing cool air to come in through the bottom and warm air to go out through the top; although permitting only half of the window area to be open, ventilation control is good. Modern versions of the window operate easily on springs concealed in the frame and no longer depend on counterbalancing with old-fashioned weights on ropes, which were always breaking, letting the window crash down on someone's hand.

Most double-hung windows can be cleaned, with some gymnastics, from the inside, and some can be removed from the frame for cleaning. Screens are usually on

Sliding windows are usually too cheaply manufactured to be made secure, especially if they are of thin aluminum. Wood requires some play for swelling and shrinking caused by weather.

the outside, and the windows consequently require frequent cleaning because the dust that settles on the screens splashes back on the glass during a rain.

In general, double-hung windows are much less secure than awning or casement windows because they can be opened without a crank. The small snap locks provided by the manufacturer can be opened with a knife in seconds, so an additional lock is necessary.

Single-hung Windows

This is a cheap version of the double-hung window in which only the bottom half of the window can be opened. It offers nothing additional for security and is generally not used in residential work. It is sometimes referred to as a barn sash.

Sliding Windows

These are double-hung windows on their side and have all their disadvantages but none of their advantages, from either a security or a practical standpoint. They open horizontally on tracks that must be kept clean or the windows will bind and stick; they can also do this on their own. Ventilation is fair to poor because only half of the window can be open, but with the openings

The hopper window, a combination of fixed glass and a ventilating sash hinged at the bottom and opening into the room, is not the most secure.

on the same level, higher warm air cannot escape.

Sliding windows are usually inexpensive aluminum windows and tend to rattle with the smallest breeze. Some models can be lifted out of the frames from the outside and are thus a very bad security risk. Even if they are made of wood, the play required so they can slide easily and to allow for swelling makes them noisy and easy to remove from the frame.

Cleaning can be done from the inside, but screens on the outside collect dust that streaks the windows when it rains. Many tract homes built on speculation had these windows installed high in bedroom walls to increase wall space and permit easier placement of the beds. This creates a very dangerous situation in case of fire. There should be at least one window with the sill near the floor in every bedroom.

Hopper Windows

These windows have a hinged section at the bottom that opens into the room, interfering with draperies, furniture, and the shins of the unwary. They provide very poor ventilation and are associated more with motels and air-conditioned offices than with houses.

The fixed upper portion makes them im-

A jalousie window is the least secure and most difficult of all the doors and windows to protect.

possible to clean from the inside unless they pivot or open in some other way that would increase their cost and defeat their purpose.

thin glass strips are as easily broken as they are simple to remove.

Jalousie Windows
Jalousie doors and windows consist of narrow strips of glass set in horizontal series within a frame. The jalousies provide maximum ventilation and are opened and closed with a gear and lever. They can be left open during a rain.

Insofar as security goes, jalousie doors and windows are practically useless. The

Transoms
In these days of high air-conditioning costs and higher crime rates, you have to choose between locking the windows at night and paying prohibitive electric bills, or opening the windows and taking a chance on waking in the middle of the night with a knife-wielding stranger standing over you.

Transoms are windows over either other windows or doors, and can be operable or

One form of transom windows on the ground floor of Hardwick Hall, started in 1590 in Derbyshire, England.

fixed. No longer used much since the standard ceiling height has been lowered to eight feet to accommodate standardized manufactured materials, the transom can be a very useful way of getting light and air into a room while still keeping all doors and lower windows locked and shuttered. Since transoms will seldom be used as a means of escape in an emergency, they can be barred if necessary, making it inconvenient for a burglar to break in whether the family is at home or not.

Transoms are good security windows at night because they provide privacy and require the use of a ladder or some help to get to. They are also effective wired to an alarm because children and household pets do not have access to them; when they are disturbed there is good reason to be warned of it.

You do not have to raise your ceilings to put in transoms. Instead, put in two sets of good secure windows, one above the other. The lower ones can be shuttered and locked at night, the smaller upper ones can be barred and left open. Many times this will cut down on the air-conditioning load in the summer, heating in winter, and still allow enough light into the room for normal usage during the day without electricity.

The old window is vulnerable to burglars and adds nothing to the design of the house.

Using the space between the top of the window and the attic joists, a new shuttered window with a transom can be installed.

MATERIALS

Window frames are made of wood or metal, with or without a vinyl-clad exterior. Regular wood windows require a lot of maintenance—painting, puttying, and reputtying—but new ones are fairly inexpensive and are available in a wide variety of designs and sizes that vary from manufacturer to manufacturer.

Vinyl-clad windows—windows with a thin coat of vinyl on the exterior side of the wood or metal—provide nothing extra in the way of security, but they do reduce the maintenance required. They do not need to be puttied, and claims are made that they do not have to be painted for some time, although estimates differ on the length of time before they need some attention. For better scale with traditional designs, the panes of glass are simulated with a removable grille of plastic or wood that snaps out for easier window cleaning. The cost is about a third more for vinyl-clad windows.

Modern wood windows with their delicate muntins dividing the glazed area into panes

The window is secured at night with the shutters closed, allowing light to enter through the transom and air through the louvers of the shutters.

are not designed for security; the muntins are easily broken and pushed aside. Old-fashioned windows with heavy muntins did obscure the view and let in less light, but they did act to slow down, if not stop, a prowler trying to break in.

Metal windows can be aluminum or steel and are available with a vinyl coating or a baked-on finish that eliminates painting. Some metal windows have eliminated the need for putty to hold the glass in place. Others use a bead on the interior so the putty cannot be scraped away and the glass

removed. Metal windows should have an insulation break in the frame so condensation does not form on the interior, staining walls and rusting the metal from the inside.

Steel is stronger than aluminum, but of course it will rust if it is not prefinished at the factory or kept painted. A heavy steel awning or casement window divided into small panes welded into place, operated with a gear, and fitted with a keyed dead bolt is about the most secure window you can install.

Aluminum windows are not as secure as steel and can pit and deteriorate in areas with industrial fumes in the air or from salt in the air if you live near the shore. Thin aluminum can be broken, twisted, or jimmied so easily that aluminum frames are not the deterrent to breaking and entering that good wood or steel frames are.

The cost of metal-framed windows can vary from the cheapest aluminum sliding window, which can cost less than wood, to the most expensive steel with a baked-on or vinyl finish, which can cost more than twice as much as wood-framed windows.

Before there was widespread use of glass in windows, the openings were covered with woven mats or with parchment, oiled linen, or paper, and shutters were closed at night. By the fifteenth century glass began to appear in houses in northern Europe. However, it was used only in the upper section of the window, and in bad weather the shutters on the lower section were kept tightly closed. In England it was still considered an expensive French luxury, but by the time the first settlers came to North America in 1620, glass was used in small leaded panes in most houses. However, glass remained, for the colonialists at any rate, almost prohibitively expensive, not only because of the distance it had to be brought, but because the king put an extra tax on every pane.

Well, we still have unjust taxation, but lots of relatively inexpensive glass. There are more than a dozen different kinds of glass for all purposes from picture glass, the cheapest, to bulletproof glass, the most expensive.

Glass Block

Glass block is one of the most secure ways to light an interior for maximum privacy. The blocks can be interspersed with vents, grilles, or sections that open for ventilation. The double-walled blocks are hollow and provide insulation value equal to or better than that of insulating glass. An experienced crew should be used to erect a wall, especially when ventilating fans or windows are included in the design.

Glass block costs about six times as much as plate glass.

Sheet Glass

This is the least expensive, starting with the $1/16$-inch picture glass used to frame your high-school diploma, to $3/32$-inch single-strength window glass used in small pieces, through $1/4$-inch glass used for regular residential glazing. The smaller the size, the less noticeable is the distortion caused by the uneven surface of the glass.

Sheet glass provides no security in itself and should never be used where it is likely to be under any unexpected stress. It can be dangerous when shattered. It should never be used in doors or in large pieces.

Float Glass

This is simply glass manufactured by a process in which the glass is formed by floating it on the surface of molten tin. It is not polished and comes in a standard $1/4$-inch thickness used only for residential glazing. Its only advantage over sheet glass is that it produces fewer distortions.

Plate Glass

Plate glass is ground and polished after it is rolled and can be used for windows, table tops, and mirrors. It comes in thicknesses ranging from $1/8$ inch to 1 inch thick and in shades of gray and bronze for controlling heat from the sun and glare.

Plate glass has no security advantage whatsoever in the smaller thicknesses and a sheet a half inch thick, four feet wide, and seven feet high would weigh well over 190 pounds, making it impractical for residential use and extremely dangerous if shattered. A heavy sharp piece could sever a finger or a hand.

Tempered Glass

This is—and should be—required by law in all sliding glass doors. Tempered glass is made from glass that has its strength increased by heating and then suddenly cooling it. Tempered glass is three to five times as strong as regular glass and pulverizes when damaged rather than shattering into sharp heavy pieces. For this reason, it cannot be cut and must be manufactured in exact sizes.

For safety as well as security reasons, tempered, not "heat-strengthened," glass should be used in all glass doors and in all window walls. It costs only twice as much as plate glass.

Laminated Glass

This is similar to the safety glass used in automobiles, but it can be thicker for use in homes. Laminated glass is made by sandwiching plastic between two layers of glass under high pressure and heat. When the glass is broken, it sticks to the plastic. The plastic can be tinted for light and heat control, and the thicker the plastic the better the insulation against sound penetration.

Of course, as anyone who owns an automobile knows, laminated glass can be broken, but using a combination of tempered and laminated glass will produce a glass that will not be easy to break. "Bullet-resisting" glass is laminated glass in three to five layers and in thicknesses from ¾ inch to three inches. Because of the cost and the weight, bullet-resisting glass is not practical for the average home.

The thicker the glass laminate, the harder it will be and the more difficult to break. It is sold under various trade names by the manufacturers of glass. Costs run from eight to ten times more than that of plate glass per square foot.

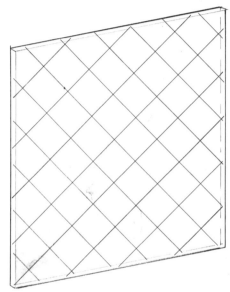

Wire glass is simply a secure glass with wire of various thicknesses embedded in it. The glass can be broken but the wire can still prevent entry.

Wire Glass

Not usually considered for residential construction, heavy wire glass will offer some security protection. It is not impossible to break through but, if the wire is heavy enough, it will certainly slow someone down. Not only does it make a lot of noise when broken, thus alerting you and your neighbors that someone is breaking in, but if accidentally broken the pieces of glass will cling to the wire where they cannot cause serious injury.

Wire glass is usually thought of for use in skylights where there could be a danger from falling tree branches and where light, not aesthetics, is important. Since the glass does not have to be of the best quality, the cost of wire glass is only twice that of regular plate.

Insulating Glass

This is not a special kind of glass but simply two sheets of glass separated by a hermetically sealed air space. It is widely used in all styles of windows and doors. Insulating glass has no security value of itself and breaking through it will depend on the glass used. Its cost is about five times that of plate.

Plastic Glass

There are various plastics used for window glazing that can be very tough to break. Plastic can be a good security precaution, but some of the larger sheets used in sliding glass doors, for instance, are so flexible they can simply be pushed out of the frame. Since they will not usually break under these conditions, it is a silent process much to the intruder's advantage. You want to make anyone breaking in take as much time and make as much noise as possible.

Other disadvantages to the plastic glass are that it scratches easily and irreparably, is affected by some acids and industrial fumes, and can discolor and disintegrate if these, combined with sun and saltwater, are in the air. The plastic is so delicate that it is delivered to the building site covered by a protective coat of heavy paper with explicit instructions that the paper not be removed until the plastic is installed and all finishing work around it has been completed.

The plastic may be tough to break through, but check to see how easy it is to burn through. Most manufacturers claim that plastic glass will not support fire or is self-extinguishing. Although this can be true, burglars have been known to burn their way through quickly and silently with an inexpensive blow torch without fear of spreading the fire or of attracting attention.

Wood and iron shutters, such as these in a house in Florence overlooking an atrium well into which a water jug could be lowered, were used during the Renaissance.

Another danger of using plastic materials, whether for glazing material, draperies, carpets, or foam rubber padding, is that in burning it produces toxic fumes that are much more dangerous than the fire itself. If you do use plastic for glazing, use it only in areas where security is a problem, such as sidelights beside the front door or small basement windows, not on vast and continuous window walls.

The plastic glass costs four to five times as much as plate glass.

Proprietary Glass

These are special types of chemically tempered glass, sold under various brand names, that can be ten, fifteen, or even twenty times as tough to break as regular glass. They can be used for security installations if the glass is thick enough not to bend out of the frame and cannot be burned out.

SHUTTERS

Welcome back the shutter. They have been used for thousands of years to make our homes more secure and more attractive at the same time. Not the cheap little false shutters builders nailed on each side of the picture windows of thirty years ago in an effort to get something on the wall to look at besides the bad lines of the house, but the tough working shutters that always break loose and bang against the side of the house on a foggy stormy night just as the power

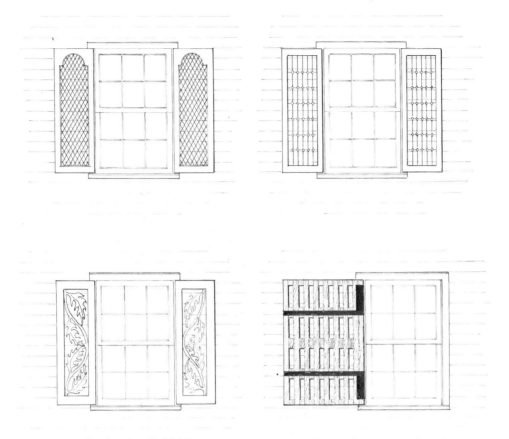

Shutters do not have to be standard lumberyard products and can provide as much shade and ventilation as you want with panels filled with heavy wire, aluminum grilles, standard wrought iron available at hardware stores, or open wood-product grilles. Shutters do not have to be double. The one shown lower right is made with two-by-fours bolted together and hung with heavy iron hinges.

goes off and your wife sees "something funny" on the lawn.

Shutters can look great, but they do not look well on all houses or work well on all windows. You should be able to open and close shutters from inside the house. This can be done with only three kinds of windows, and not with equal ease: double-hung, sliding, and some casement windows.

Double-hung windows work very well with shutters, although the screen has to be moved out of the way. With sliding windows, you can slide windows and screens to one side, close the one shutter, then move the windows and screens to the other side to close the second shutter. If the casement window swings in, as few do, there is no problem, but if it cranks out, there is no way

to get the shutter closed from inside the house.

Fixed windows, awning, hopper, and jalousie windows should not have shutters on them and you will have to resort to grilles or interior shutters for these, not only because you would have to go outdoors to secure them, which can be risky, but because shutters with these windows look like the devil.

A shutter is nothing more than a locked door over a window. Just as the entrance establishes the character of your house, shutters are a strong influence in determining the character of the facade. Besides giving you extra security, shutters can help you control the temperature in the house. The insulating value of wood shutters keeping

A grille over a corner window on an ancient house in Antigua, Guatemala, providing security, privacy, and shade from the intense sun.

cold air and wind off your windows in winter and in keeping the sun and warm air out in summer is considerable, and the fuel savings can be too.

You do not have to go around opening and closing shutters every morning and night. Bedroom window shutters on the second floor have traditionally been louvered so when closed at night they will allow fresh air to circulate through the rooms. First-floor windows, always a weak link in security efforts, have traditionally been shuttered with solid panels, perhaps with a crescent moon, a star, or a pine tree cut out of the panel, but only to allow a bit of light to filter into the room so you can find your way around in the closed-up and secure first-floor.

Operable shutters are usually made of wood because that is the easiest material to work with. They do not have to be solid wood. You can have a wood frame with a decorative metal grille set into it, or a metal frame with the center section of plastic or reinforced glass or metal grille. You do not have to have expensive lumber-mill shutters. They can be made of plank or waterproof half-inch exterior-grade plywood. What they must be is snug and easily opened from the interior but not the exterior of the house.

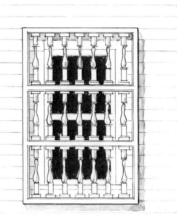

Wooden grilles can be made of old stair balusters or any number of turned spindles available in lumber yards and hardware stores.

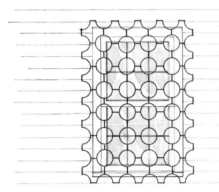
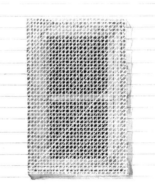

Metal grilles can be wrought-iron or heavy radiator grilles that are available in dozens of patterns. They could also be used as panels for shutters.

INTERIOR SHUTTERS

If you do not want or cannot fit exterior shutters on your windows, you can use interior shutters. These too have been used for years and do not have to be the lightweight decorator shutters pictured in advertisements for things like kitchen cabinets. Interior shutters can be almost as secure as shutters on the outside of the house, although it is preferable not to allow an intruder to get that far. Because of the space required to open and fold the shutters away to the side for storage, interior shutters are made in small sections hinged together. This also limits the size of the hardware and the screws or bolts used to fasten the hardware to the shutter, so it will be somewhat flimsier than exterior hardware.

Interior shutters work rather awkwardly on all but fixed and double-hung windows because of the cranks and other hardware used to operate casement, awning, and jalousie windows. However, you can extend the hardware and cut the solid shutter around it.

Use the heaviest lumber you can, remembering that a half-inch panel of plywood is much harder to break through and much stronger than a board of the same thickness.

A metal grille copied from the seventeenth-century "Place of the Hummingbird" in Huitziltepec, Mexico, gives architectural character to the facade and security to ground-floor windows.

Plywood is three or more sheets of wood glued together with the grain running in alternate directions so that it is more difficult to crack and less likely to warp.

A two-by-four, held tight by a set of U-shaped brackets, can be dropped over each set of shutters to prevent their being pushed in, as lighter panels and hardware can easily be.

WINDOW GRILLES

Steel bars do not a prison make, and a metal grille over your window does not have to turn your house into a jail. Again, the most important element in the protection given to your windows is to make sure that, while others cannot get in, your family can get out quickly in an emergency and not be trapped.

There are many grilles available, from handmade Spanish grilles to mass-produced commercial and industrial grilles. The U.S. government recommends that wire mesh protection over windows be a minimum of ⅛ inch in diameter and the space between a maximum of two inches. If bars are used, the government recommends they be ¾ inch in diameter and not more than five inches apart, set three inches into masonry. However, this five inches is a bit arbitrary, since much depends on the design of the grille.

The grille does not have to be made of metal; it could be wood, reinforced concrete, or reinforced plastic. Probably nothing quite as light as lattice or lath would be suitable, but again everything depends on the design.

Woven wire mesh window guards are manufactured in stainless steel, aluminum, brass, bronze, and other metals. They are hinged and locked with a padlock fitting. Because of this, they should be used only on the inside of windows, where they cannot be tampered with. The mesh is too closely

A second-floor window can be made safer and more interesting with projected grillework providing a space for growing plants and perhaps a quiet few minutes before retiring for the night.

spaced to reach through. Padlocks and combination locks are unwise, because keys can be lost and combinations forgotten in emergencies. A shielded bolt can keep the window guard in place.

A grille or bars can cover the window, or they can be set away from the wall to form a protective arbor or balcony to keep prowlers completely away from the window. A form of this was used in India and China on upper floors to seclude the women's quarters, sometimes using elaborate tracery of marble and plaster.

On the ground floor such an expanded grille or cage could be built on a concrete slab or on a foundation wall 36 inches deep to discourage digging under it to gain access. On upper floors the enclosed balcony should have a structural floor equal to that of any porch, because it is inevitable that children and adults will use it either as a convenient perch to clean windows or, if it is as attractive as it should be, as a place to sit and take the air.

If it is as large as a small balcony, the projecting grille should have a hinged and

Basement windows can be secured by metal grilles, but they must extend at least 3 inches into the masonry. A grille in the light well will also act as a deterrent, but only if it covers a sufficient area of the window to make it too small for entry.

latched escape window that can be released from inside the room. This will keep outsiders from tampering with it but allow family members to release it before opening the window in an emergency. Alternatively, it might have a hinged floor, again controllable from the inside of the house at a location next to the window, that can drop down to form an escape ladder in case of fire.

The projecting grille could also take the form of a miniature greenhouse, strong enough to support a few plants, but not enough to support the weight of an intruder.

BASEMENT WINDOWS

Basement windows, lying close to or sunk below the grade, are much more difficult to secure than ground-floor windows. Conventional ground-floor windows can be as accessible, but they are not—or should not be—hidden by shrubbery and are treated as part of the architectural facade, as basement windows seldom are. It is possible to hide behind anything built or planted around basement windows or even to fall into the light well opening if unprotected.

Most basement windows are small metal rectangles fitting precisely between standard concrete blocks or in other masonry. If they are above grade they can be protected by a grille or exterior or interior shutters. The interior shutters are the least secure, although the hardest to get to. Since these windows offer very poor means of escape in case of emergency because they are high on the interior wall, the interior grille or shutter can

First-floor windows can be protected with metal grilles, adding style and character to the house. The double-hung window grille (left) must be set far enough away so the window can be cleaned. A casement window that swings out can be protected by a projected grille and window box.

be made of sturdy material anchored to the wall so that it would be difficult to push in.

If these small basement windows are set partly or wholly below grade surrounded by a light well, they are difficult to secure because the light well itself can give a certain amount of cover to an intruder. If the windows are small enough, they can make an entry uncomfortable, but they will also permit little light and air into the basement, thus defeating their prime function.

Semidome grilles covering the window and the well are not very successful because the light well must be cleaned. This is also the objection to a flat grille set in concrete, although, of the two, the latter is preferable because it can cut the exposed window area down by half or more. Both create the problem of providing space for field mice and

other rodents and adding to the dampness of the basement.

Plastic domes can be fitted over the window and the light well allowing light to enter but cutting off the air. This, plus the fact that they can be shattered or removed, makes them a dubious choice.

Rather than be bothered with the small inconvenient windows and the light wells surrounding them, you can enlarge both until they are worthwhile as sources of light and ventilation, or eliminate them entirely and put in fixed ventilating grilles too small to permit entry even if they are pried loose.

These small standard basement windows can be eliminated or replaced inasmuch as they should never be regarded as a means of escape. Every basement should, however, have two means of exit, at least one directly

The house opposite, before remodeling.

to the exterior and a second through the house above. This is a rule that should never be ignored regardless of how it affects the design of the remodeling.

FIRST-FLOOR WINDOWS

Small windows on the first floor can be protected with either a shutter or a grille that is permanent if they are not in strategic rooms and another means of escape is available. Large windows can be secured with two sets of shutters, one covering the lower portion of the window and another on the top section, left open to admit light without being an invitation to a casual prowler who decides to take advantage of an easy situation.

For very large windows, sliding glass doors, and whole walls of glass, heavy steel screens or grilles that roll up out of the way, much the same as those used on stores and banks, can be used if the installation warrants. These should be equipped with alarms and be electrically and manually operated.

Some windows—double-hung, for instance—lend themselves better than others to steel grilles just as some architectural styles—such as Spanish—get along with grilles over the windows better than others. American colonial styles can look a bit strained with a steel grille covering the win-

First-floor windows can be made secure by excavating to the basement level. At the same time, the basement has been opened up to light and air with new sliding glass doors, all protected by a masonry and wrought-iron fence. A balcony off the living room windows acts as a platform for cleaning and shades the basement windows.

dows, although some others can take on a Spanish character simply by the addition of a Spanish grille and hardware on the doors and windows. The disadvantage of grilles is that they must be removed or opened for window cleaning.

Windows that open out can be protected with a trellised arbor projecting from the facade. The effectiveness of the arbor can be increased as far as security goes and the im-

pact of its severity lessened if thorny climbing roses are encouraged to twine through the arbor.

Other large first-floor windows, especially bedroom windows, can be protected without cutting off the light, air, and view by removing the earth from the basement wall to a depth of eight feet or more, and actually constructing something similar to the ancient moat, creating a basement terrace.

First-floor and second-floor windows can be secured with a continous metal grille without acting as a ladder which a prowler could climb. The second-floor grille must be operable so no one can be trapped inside in case of a fire.

This can open basement areas to light and air, and protect first-floor windows at the same time. In effect, it makes bedroom windows in a one-story house almost as safe as second-floor windows, and they can be left open safely at night for ventilation. A fence will have to be built around the basement courtyard or the retaining wall made higher to prevent stray animals and children from falling in. Small balconies can project from floor-length windows to make the windows easier to clean and for safety.

Before a basement courtyard is planned at a level much below grade, the site should be thoroughly investigated to be sure there are no walls, power or water lines, sewers, or other obstructions preventing excavation below the basement for the outsized light well area.

SECOND-FLOOR WINDOWS

Do not suppose that just because windows are a story or more above the ground that they are perfectly safe from professional burglars. People can get a false sense of security about upper windows, locking basement and first-floor windows and leaving second-floor and attic windows unlocked. Of course, they are safer from prowlers, but second-floor windows are often used to gain entrance into a house. This is especially true if they are adjacent to a lower roof and are out of sight of the street and neighbors. Even if the windows are visible, few neighbors or policemen will check or question professional-appearing window cleaners, roofers, painters, or television antenna crews who arrive in clean overalls, with tools and a truck bearing a fictitious company name. Of course, if the second-floor windows are out of sight, most of them can be reached simply by driving a van or truck under them and using the roof of the vehicle to stand on.

If professional burglars want to get into your house, almost nothing—not alarms, bars, moats—will stop them from eventually breaking in. After all, banks have been designed for years to prevent robbers from stealing their money, but banks are still being robbed. You are not looking to live in a fortress, but to prevent dope addicts, the crazies, juvenile delinquents, vandals, and even roving bands of bored children from taking advantage of your lack of prevention.

If you have alarms on first-floor windows, have them on second-floor and attic windows too. If this is not practical, unbreakable glass in small but heavy steel frames can be used along with good locks.

Thick wooden shutters can be used if they are easily unlocked from inside, but remember that shutters are only a security measure when they are closed. They will cut down on light and ventilation in the bedrooms, but they do not have to plunge the room into breathless darkness. Any number of small sturdy grilles and louvers, or even just holes, can be placed in shutters so that light and air can still enter when the shutters are closed and locked. Second-floor bedrooms are occupied mostly at night when electricity must be used for light anyway, so you will use very little more, and this can be made up in the savings on fuel and air-conditioning costs that the additional insulation the shutters give will provide.

Fixed permanent grilles should not be used on second-floor bedroom windows. Often in a fire the bedroom window can be the only means of escape and the grille can prevent occupants from getting out or rescuers from reaching them.

Windows on upper floors can be secured with an interior metal grille that slides over the window from a container at the top of the window. Narrow slits in the grille can be regulated for more or less light and air and controlled manually or electrically.

Luxurious highrise apartments and condominiums in close proximity to deteriorating neighborhoods are more prone to attempted break-ins. Neither the apartments nor the neighborhoods themselves are safe.

Chapter Eleven

Apartments and Condominiums

Large cities are not the only places people live in apartments and condominiums. However, the most numerous, the largest, most expensive, and most burglarized apartment houses are in or near urban centers close to and easily accessible from deteriorating areas spawning crime.

New York City is always held to be the best and worst of everything, and it has often been claimed that what happens there eventually seeps into the rest of the country. New York City has more than 100,000 known heroin addicts who require $4 million a day to support their addiction—$1.5 billion a year that they must steal. And drug addicts are not the only people committing crimes.

The rate per 100,000 population for burglary alone in New York City is 2,178, but for Detroit the figure is 2,730, for Newark 2,846, and for our nation's capital, Washington, D.C., the figure is 3,031. These figures do not include robbery, which is defined as stealing or taking anything of value by force or violence, or other crimes.

There is a burglary, defined as breaking and entering, every 13 seconds, 54 percent of them committed by children under eighteen, many of them on drugs other than heroin, who have committed 100 to 150 burglaries each. Fewer than one burglary in five is solved. Each year we grow a new crop of criminals to add to the criminals put back on the street—60 percent of all those released from jail are arrested again within four years and 69 percent of all people paroled are rearrested.

Because of zoning ordinances separating living and working areas in cities and towns and suburbs, most apartments are broken into during the day when, in the majority of cases, people are away working or shopping. Most suburban houses are broken into at night when the streets are deserted and everyone is asleep. Crime is not a problem in this country alone, but it is really quite sad that a freedom-loving nation such as ours is leading the advance full circle back to a fortressed living style common in the Dark Ages of Europe. Keeping his clients safe in their own homes and apartments is one of the biggest problems an architect is presented with today.

Being poor is no guarantee of not being robbed. If you have a house or an apartment to live in, a roof over your head of any kind, you can have more than someone else who decides he wants it and can take it away from you.

It was only in July of 1972 that a multi-million-dollar government-sponsored low-income apartment development in St. Louis, called the Pruitt-Igoe Development, had to be blown up because the huge apartment complex was the object of so much crime that, even with government assistance, people refused to live there and police and firemen were afraid to go to their aid.

Hiring the best armed guards available, living in only the best-protected and most exclusive neighborhood can minimize the likelihood of your being victimized by a prowler roaming the area looking for an opportunity to rob you, but it can also stamp you as a target with something worth stealing. It makes more sense for a crook to risk his neck breaking into a condominium on Palm Beach's exclusive South Ocean Road than into a one-room apartment across the bridge on Dixie Highway in Lake Worth.

Remember, too, that some criminals thrive on the excitement and danger of the possibility of being caught. They also enjoy the gamesmanship involved in outwitting the most ingenious devices and tightest security controls that can be designed.

Once you buy a condominium or rent an apartment, there is little you can do about the neighborhood or your neighbors. Do not take the real estate agent's word for the safety of the area or the security system of the apartment. The apartment may be available because the neighborhood is deteriorating so rapidly and the building is so badly managed everyone wants to move out. Tenants are not going to give you, a stranger, information concerning their security system or lack of it.

Go talk to the police. A telephone call will not do. Go to the station, identify yourself, and explain your intention. Ask about the incidence of crime in the neighborhood, the number of crimes and break-ins reported for the building—not only burglaries, but also robberies—the false alarms, vandalism, family and tenant arguments, wild parties, and noisy television sets. If there are numerous calls to the police for inconsequential family or neighborhood squabbles —if they go to the same address several times a week to ask someone to turn down the *Tonight Show* or to tell 3-C he cannot walk his dog under 2-B's window—the police are less likely to risk life and limb speeding in response to a really serious call.

FIRST-FLOOR AND GARDEN APARTMENTS

If you live alone or are going to be alone for periods of time, first-floor and garden apartments are a bad risk. They are too accessible to the street on the exterior and to too many people on the interior of the apartment house. They can also be uncomfortable to live in, and although they may seem ideal for the handicapped, they are not because their windows are on the street. In an intimate suburban neighborhood this is fine, but in a big city you cannot sit and watch the movement and activity on the street without being on display yourself.

You may not want to run the air-conditioning all summer to be cool, but you may have to in order to keep out the dust

The entrance to an apartment or condominium should be separated from the public sidewalk and street by a clearly defined area. This attended lobby door opens from the exterior only with a key and is sheltered with a canvas awning.

and noise. With or without air-conditioning, you can be forced to keep the draperies drawn for privacy most of the time, creating a dark, sunless interior. This can make any apartment depressing and unpleasant to live in, and more expensive if you must use electricity in order to see.

Every first-floor and garden apartment should have a heavy grille or bars over each window. Regular glass should be replaced with laminated or break-resistant glass. An air-conditioner placed in a double-hung window without a protective grille over it should be removed and installed through the wall, since units can be removed to gain entrance to the apartment.

THE STREET

You cannot remodel the street, but before you rent an apartment or buy a condominium you can see if the street itself is secure. It should not be an open—that is, unbarricaded—dead-end street; no police cars will be driving through for surveillance. True, a dead-end street will not be used by honest people who have no business there, but you do not have to be concerned about honest people.

The street should be well lighted, the trees should be trimmed to permit the light to fall on the sidewalk without casting shadows.

Automobile parking should not be permitted after dusk. The street is built for public transportation, not to be a parking facility.

There should be no place for strangers to hide at night between parked cars, in small alleys, between buildings, behind garbage bins, or in unlighted recessed entrances to shops or buildings.

The sidewalk in front of the apartment building should be divided into two well-demarcated sections between the curb and the door of the apartment house so that there is a clearly defined transition between the public sidewalk and the apartment grounds. There should be a wall, fence, or steps so there is no mistaking the boundary line. Pressure-sensitive mats here should alert a doorman or anyone in the lobby when this symbolic barrier has been crossed.

There should be no overgrown foundation planting anywhere at all on the entrance side of the apartment where someone could hide in the shadows. The street side of the building should be brightly lighted at night.

THE LOBBY

Every safe apartment house with more than five or six units will have a lobby, and one with more than twelve to fifteen units should have a resident manager and limited and controlled access. There can be many emergency exits in an apartment house, but there should be only one lobby and only controlled entrances to it.

In groups of five or six apartments, the residents get to know and recognize each other and are aware if anything suspicious occurs. Larger apartment complexes need someone living there who can recognize tenants, be on hand to receive packages, to maintain the lobby, and to solve electric and plumbing problems.

Beware of apartment houses with a high proportion of older children because they are the group least concerned with security and are rarely, if ever, victimized. A high teenage population can defeat the best security system simply because it is not in their interest to maintain it. They are also the age group most commonly arrested for burglary, robbery, and assault.

From the sidewalk on the outside of the apartment house you should have a clear and unobstructed view of the entire lobby and the elevators before you enter. There should be no hidden pockets or unlighted recesses where someone could hide. Every corner of the lobby should be brightly lighted.

At night the entrance lobby should be brightly lighted with no hidden corners that cannot be observed from the exterior. The doorman's desk is opposite the door, providing a clear view of the mail boxes on the left and the elevator doors on the right.

If there is a doorman's station, it should be directly in front of the door so that everyone going in and out of the building must pass it. He should have a clear view of mailboxes, elevator doors, and panel.

The mailboxes should face the lobby and not be around a corner where they cannot be seen from the door. Do not put your full name on the mailbox. Use only initials with your surnames and if you live alone list a fictitious name along with yours. This can make a stranger think that even though you are out of town, the apartment is still occupied.

Every apartment house is safer with a doorman stationed in the lobby at all times. If tenants insist that he take time away from the door to deliver packages and carry groceries, a full-time porter should be hired. The doorman should be able to communicate directly with the tenants through an intercom system located at his desk.

Avoid automatic elevators unless there is a doorman on duty. If there is an underground garage make sure the elevator cannot bypass the lobby and continue to upper floors. An apartment garage also calls for closed-circuit television in the garage and in the ceiling of the elevator. The camera should be mounted on the roof of the cab.

CLOSED-CIRCUIT TELEVISION

Many apartments and condominiums have CCTV systems installed with cameras at all entrances and exits, lobbies, corridors, and elevators. CCTV is expensive to have installed and can be a deterrent, but it is only as good and as reliable as the personnel monitoring the system.

THE HALLWAY

The corridors leading to the apartment from the elevator should be straight, with no breaks or hiding places in them. The lighting should be bright, recessed, and protected so that no one except a maintenance man can get into the fixtures to remove the bulbs. You do not want to take a chance on arriving home alone in the evening to a dark hallway. If this should happen, return to the elevator and the lobby immediately.

The corridor should have fire extinguishers and fire hoses at intervals along the wall. On each fire extinguisher there should be a tag with the date and name of the inspector who checked it to see if it was in working order.

The width and length of the hall are determined by law, as are the number and locations of fire stairs. You should never have to walk more than 100 feet from your apartment door to the fire exit. The exit must be indicated with a lighted exit sign that has a battery-operated emergency power source.

The corridors should be protected from fire with sprinklers and be equipped with smoke detectors. There should also be smoke detectors in every apartment.

The doors of the fire stair should be equipped with panic hardware on the corridor side and open into the stairwell. They should close and lock automatically, and the stair side of the door should have no hardware—the fire stair should not be used to visit from one floor to another.

Exits from the fire stair should be limited to the roof at the top and to the exterior on the ground floor. Shortcuts to the street or parking lot via the stair should be discouraged by making the ground-floor exit inconvenient for anything except escape. Uncooperative tenants can often use these shortcuts, making illegal entry easier because they neglect to make sure the doors are properly closed and locked. Children can also leave fire stair doors propped open to make entry easier in an effort to get back and forth between their apartment and play areas quickly.

The exit to the roof should never be locked or capable of being locked. The roof exit should be equipped with an alarm, connected to the fire station, that will go off if the door is opened. To prevent false alarms, a large sign on the door should indicate that the door is wired to an alarm.

THE APARTMENT

The door to the apartment should be metal, metal-covered wood or, in some cases, solid wood, at least two inches thick, swinging into the apartment. The door frame should be metal or metal-covered wood. If the frame is metal, the interior of the frame should be filled with cement grout that will withstand crushing around the strike plate so the frame cannot be jimmied away from the plate and lock.

The door should fit tightly within rabbeted jambs and be fitted with a combination peephole and intercom so you can see and question anyone at the door. It should also have a keyed chain lock so you can open it slightly to receive small packages and special delivery mail. These locks should never be depended on if the door is left open for air

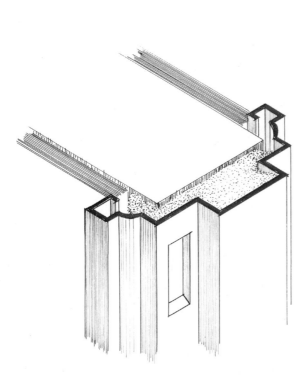

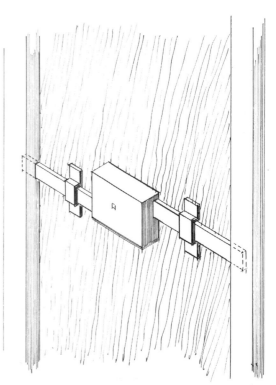

A hollow metal door frame should replace wood jambs with cement grout reinforcing to prevent the frame from being bent out of shape and allowing the door to be forced away from the lock.

A double bar lock, used to increase the strength of a door, is only effective if the bars lock into heavy metal jambs. The cylinder lock on the exterior should be protected by an escutcheon plate to prevent forcible removal.

circulation because they are quite easily forced open with a karate kick, but they are useful if you are sure the mailman or delivery man is legitimate and means no harm.

The door should also be equipped with a heavy mortise lock with a dead bolt. A second dead bolt is advisable. If you rent, the apartment manager may not permit you to change the lock, so have your own added to the door. If the manager insists on having a passkey in case of emergency, give it to him in a sealed and taped envelope with your name on it. Then no one can open the envelope, have a duplicate key made, and replace your key without making it obvious the envelope has been tampered with.

If you buy a condominium and the door and locks are not suitable, buy a new door frame, door, and locks. Temporary additional security can be provided on the weak door by a buttress door lock.

In addition to the door from the hallway to the apartment, the biggest security problem in most apartments is the sliding glass door to the terrace. This is true of French and sliding glass doors almost anywhere.

Terraces on the ground floor can be approached directly by prowlers and must be protected. Second-floor terraces are only slightly more secure. On the ground floor, entry and exit can be quick and easy. High foundation planting around the terrace for the tenant's privacy can also screen a prowler and at the same time give him a chance to study the apartment and the occupants' habits. Sometimes this planting cannot be removed or cut back because it is the property of the apartment house or condominium, and it can also be a problem if you rent because you may not want to invest in costly, however attractive, security precautions.

A ground-floor terrace of an apartment can be protected with a wall and be made to appear larger by building a false gate on one wall and filling it with exterior mirror to reflect and double the size.

The planting used to screen the terrace for privacy can be made more dense for at least the part of the year when you want to use the terrace by planting quick-growing annual vines such as morning glories or moon vine—even squash or cucumbers—and letting them grow up a high barbed-wire trellis surrounding the terrace. Of course the barbed wire can be cut, but this takes time and is obvious. The wire can be connected to an alarm to alert you if it is tampered with.

If you own your own apartment in a condominium and are permitted to make security alterations, you can take the same measure or erect a permanent chain-link or other type of fence, a concrete block wall, either solid or pierced, or use glass block. Any of these fences or walls topped with barbed wire, disguised and reinforced with innocent-looking roses, whose thorns themselves are a wise precaution, will increase the security of a terrace. Any of them can be wired to an alarm.

Top-floor terraces can be made more secure from intruders from the roof with a heavy metal awning.

If enclosing the already small terrace is discouraging, the space can be made to feel much larger and more interesting with exterior mirrors. The mirror can be used across the entire surface of one or more walls, or you can create an expansive atmosphere by framing the mirror with a gate structure, giving the appearance that the terrace is only the entrance to a much larger garden.

Generally, glassing in the terrace to make it into a porch will rob you of the advantage of having outdoor living space. The use of jalousies or conventional glazing only compounds the security problem in a ground-floor apartment because they are easy to get through and will hide the intruder.

Terraces on the top floor of an apartment house are vulnerable to access from the roof. The fire stair must exit to the roof by code. Too often tenants or children using the fire stair for a shortcut will be careless about closing the door or will even invite prowlers by propping it open. An accomplice working

Apartment and condominium terraces can be secured from adjacent terraces inexpensively by simply screening them off with chain-link fencing softened with climbing roses.

inside the building can also open the ground-floor exit to allow a burglar to enter. After gaining access to the roof, a prowler can drop to a terrace or let himself down to it using a rope or an extra-long belt from his pants.

Top-floor terraces can be made more secure by covering them with awnings of glass or plastic. If someone should drop to the awning from the apartment house roof, it would not support his weight and could be wired to sound an alarm. A steeply sloped structural roof, over 45 degrees, would also be too dangerous to drop to because a prowler could not get a foothold and would roll over the edge.

When the terrace is roofed by the apartment house roof, the edge can be extended with a permanent awning that increases the distance, and therefore the danger, a prowler must face to swing out over the edge to gain access. Pressure-sensitive tape or mats on the roof or awning will sound an alarm if anyone walks on them.

An awning in combination with shutters, sliding ventilating panels, or jalousies, while very insecure at ground level, is difficult to tamper with from the outside on, say, the twentieth floor.

The parapet above the terrace could be protected by a chain-link fence, which could also be connected to an alarm in case it was tampered with. However, the sheer improbability of successfully climbing up and over or cutting through a fence a number of stories in the air would discourage all but the most determined.

All terraces are vulnerable from the terrace directly above. If your upstairs neighbors are away, it is wise to know about it. Someone might be tempted to break into their apartment with the thought of using yours for escape if interrupted during the burglary.

On intermediate levels of a building, adjacent terraces often provide excellent entry to apartments. This is basically a problem of design created by an architect unconcerned about security. If the wall dividing your terrace from your neighbor's does not extend to the ceiling and three feet beyond the terrace railing, you have a security problem. You may know and trust your neighbors, but you cannot know when they may walk in on a burglar, and you do not want to be in between when some insane escapee is shooting at the police chasing him.

Extend the separating wall out three feet beyond the terrace railing and make sure that no one can get over or under it. If this cannot be done in a structural way because of building codes or zoning ordinances, or simply because "it will spoil the looks of the building" in the eyes of the management, extend the wall with barbed trellises or a solid piece of unframed tough plastic or glass, or block off the accessible railing with a piece of lightweight chicken wire strong enough to support potted plants but not a person. You can even tie bells on it that will make a racket if it's disturbed. Avoid anything that could break or fall to the street below and injure someone.

Now that you have done your best to keep prowlers off the terrace, turn your attention to the terrace door. The apartment can be further secured by all the methods used to secure French or sliding glass doors in Chapter 9—shutters, small panes of laminated glass set in a metal grid, added masonry or wood to decrease the opening size, plus locks and alarms. The terrace door is where the apartment is most vulnerable.

Small windows on the terrace of an apartment on the first, second, or top floor should have exterior grilles over them and interior shutters that can be locked. Small second-floor windows on open sides of the apartment will probably not need additional protection other than good locks if they cannot be reached from a lower roof or the top of a truck and are in full view of the street, passersby, and the police.

A central alarm system can be installed in an apartment and wired to a security company in the same way as in a private house. It can be silent, ringing only at the security company's office and at a doorman's or guard station if the apartment has one, but not in the apartment, or it can ring in the apartment, too, in an attempt to frighten the burglar away. There are a variety of alarm systems.

If you do not have a central system, at least have the best locks on the strongest doors you can afford, a panic button that will ring in the hall and alert your neighbors, an internal alarm system that will wake you in time to telephone for help if a door or window is being tampered with, and a smoke detector that will wake you in case of a fire in the apartment. Smoke detectors are better for fire than heat detectors since the latter are set to go off after the room temperature reaches 120 to 130 degrees. A fire can get a good start or smolder for a long time before the room temperature becomes that high.

The addition of a security room on the exterior is possible on either the first or second floor. The almost undiscernible door equipped with panic hardware on the interior (no hardware on the exterior) can be hinged on the bottom to provide a stair or ladder to safety.

Chapter Twelve

The Security Room

This chapter will probably not apply to the average household with growing children living at home. In the first place, these are not the houses most burglars pick to rob. There is too much activity going on, too much chance to get caught tripping over a roller skate or knocking over Humpty Dumpty, and too little to steal to make it worth the effort when the widow next door has several generations of silver in the dining room. Second, for the household in which just getting the children off to the school bus on time is a daily crisis, the simple logistics of rounding up the family and getting them into a security room would be overwhelming, especially since this must be done quickly and quietly.

Basically, the security room is meant for one- or two-person households with one bedroom, and more precisely, for women living alone, who are increasingly the objects of burglary, robbery, and assault. Women live longer than men, and usually the wealthier widows are the longer they continue to survive their husbands because they can afford the best of health care. These are the most frequent victims of crime and too often, because of their helplessness, of violent crime. The criminal simply does not want to leave them alive to identify him.

One answer—not the only one, to be sure—is a security room. People have safes to protect their jewelry and valuables—why not a safe to protect their lives?

The security room is a place to flee to when you think someone is in the house or apartment after you have taken all the precautions to make the premises safe from intruders. It should be used only to give you time to notify the police and neighbors that you need help. It must not allow an intruder to trap you inside. For this reason, the security room must have

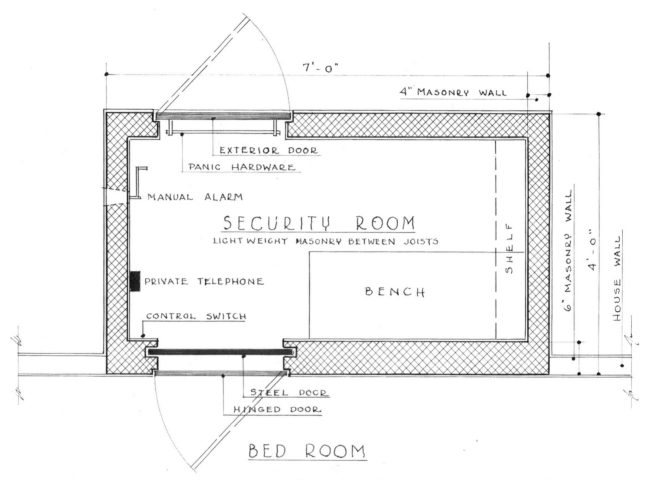

A minimum-size security room added to a bedroom. The room should have a water jug, any prescription drugs the occupant may be required to take, a flashlight, warm bathrobe, slippers, and an extra pair of eyeglasses, so the room can be entered without stopping to pick up odds and ends.

its own exit door to the outside, fitted with panic hardware. There should be no hardware on the exterior of the exit door and no way of opening it from the outside.

The security room should be off your bedroom; it could conceivably be a bathroom. However, it should never be a closet or a room that is used for storage because the one time you need it, it will be filled with boxes or unwrapped Christmas presents.

If the security room is used for any other purpose, such as a bathroom off the bed-room, it should have a regular 1¾-inch solid wood door set in rabbeted jambs. This door would be for everyday use and would not be the main source of security. It should swing out from, not into, the room, so it can be closed quickly and has no chance of interfering with the security door.

The security door is a steel door that drops from the head of the door frame and locks instantly in place. The security door should be wired to an alarm that will turn on all the lights in the house and floodlights on

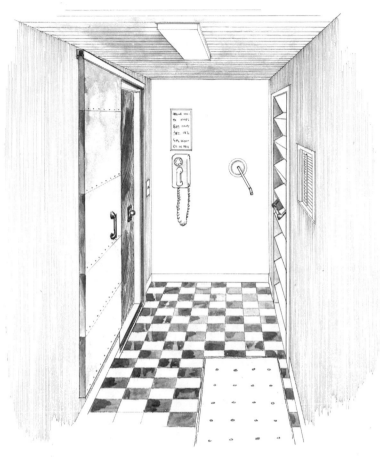

Emergency telephone numbers should be listed and mounted directly over the telephone and easily visible with a flashlight. An alternative to an overhead security door would be this sliding metal-clad door mounted on barn-door hardware that slides quickly and securely into a metal frame set into the floor and jamb. The escape door, equipped with panic hardware, can have steps built in it and be hinged from the bottom to permit easy exit if high above grade. A louvered window at the right is for additional ventilation and to observe the exterior before exiting.

the exterior and notify the police that you are in trouble. If you prefer, the closing of the steel door could automatically send an alarm only to the police station; the police would then have a much better chance of apprehending the criminal.

The walls of the security room should be four-inch concrete block or brick since standard gypsum-board partitions are easily broken through. Never keep a safe or valuables in the security room. Let the criminals have the jewelry—it can be insured and re-

placed; your life cannot be, and the room should be used only to protect you from physical violence.

The security room should also have a telephone, battery-operated lights and ventilation, and a hand-cranked siren in case there is an emergency during a power failure or the electric and telephone lines have been cut.

The room would give you the advantage of never having to come face to face with an intruder. If you heard anything suspicious in

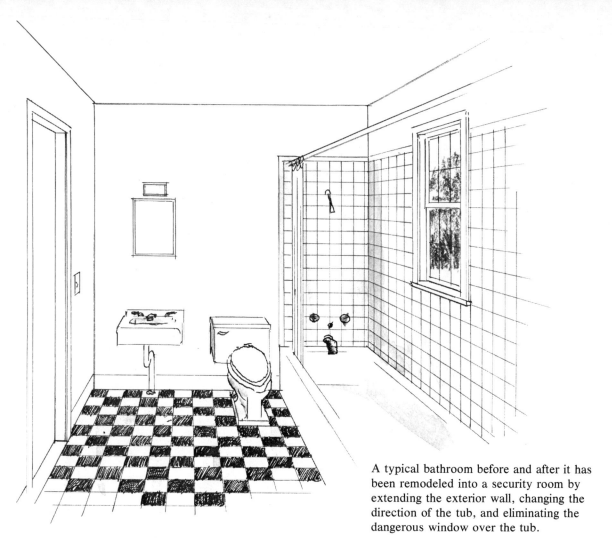

A typical bathroom before and after it has been remodeled into a security room by extending the exterior wall, changing the direction of the tub, and eliminating the dangerous window over the tub.

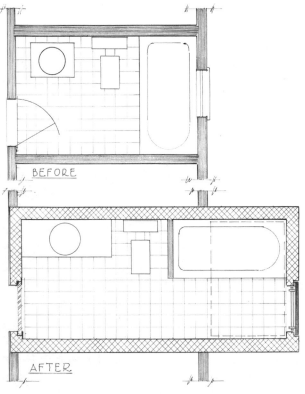

BEFORE

AFTER

the night, all you would have to do is to enter the room as quickly as possible. If the closing of the steel door silently and automatically notified the police that an intruder was in the house, they would have a chance of arriving before the criminal was aware that an alarm had been sounded and you would not be in a position to be used as a hostage. The police should be given a key to the security room so that when the door is opened you know that it is safe to leave.

In an existing house, an ideal location would be a bathroom entered only from a first-floor master bedroom. The bathroom should be on an outside wall as, again, every security room must have a means of escape;

The same bathroom extended and converted into a security room with the hinged bathroom door reversed and reinforced, roll-down steel door, exterior door with panic hardware, and counterbalanced ladder to lower occupant to safety.

a thwarted assailant could be insane enough to set fire to the house as a parting angry gesture.

Even in a two-story house, a bathroom adjoining the master bedroom can be used as a security room. The floor and walls should be fitted with lightweight masonry to resist bullets and fire. The panic door can be fitted with a counterbalanced ladder to lower a person slowly to ground level.

If a bathroom is not available or suitable for use as a security room, a room can be added to the exterior of the bedroom. It should have fireproof masonry walls and be at least three by six feet so you can lie down or sit down until help arrives if you feel faint.

The main point is to be sure you can get in the security room quickly and not be trapped there by a prowler. It would also act as an emergency exit in case of fire. This type of security could save your life because you would never face the criminal and he would not have the opportunity or necessity to harm or kill you to protect his identity.

The security room is not meant to take the place of regular alarms and protective measures, and you may never use it. But if you have to use it once, it could be the most important room in your home.

Index